Resiliency
in Schools

Resiliency in Schools

Making It Happen for Students and Educators

Nan Henderson
Mike M. Milstein

CORWIN PRESS, INC.
A Sage Publications Company
Thousand Oaks, California

For information address:

Corwin Press, Inc.
A Sage Publications Company
2455 Teller Road
Thousand Oaks, California 91320
e-mail: order@corwin.sagepub.com

SAGE Publications Ltd.
6 Bonhill Street
London EC2A 4PU
United Kingdom

SAGE Publications India Pvt. Ltd.
M-32 Market
Greater Kailash I
New Delhi 110 048 India

Printed in the United States of America

Library of Congress Cataloging-in-Publication Data

Henderson, Nan.
    Resiliency in schools: making it happen for students and
educators / Nan Henderson, Mike M. Milstein.
        p.   cm.
    Includes bibliographical references and index.
    ISBN 0-8039-6351-3 (cloth : alk. paper). — ISBN 0-8039-6352-1
(pbk. : alk. paper)
    1. Educational change—United States. 2. Resilience (Personality
trait)—United States. 3. Students—United States—Psychology.
4. Teachers—United States—Psychology. I. Milstein, Mike M.
II. Title.
LA217.2.H46   1996
370.15′8—dc20   95-53339

This book is printed on acid-free paper.

        99   00   10   9   8   7   6

Corwin Press Production Editor: S. Marlene Head

Contents

Foreword

Behavioral scientists have used the term *resilience* to describe three kinds of phenomena: (1) positive developmental outcomes among children who live in "high-risk" contexts, such as chronic poverty or parental substance abuse; (2) sustained competence under prolonged stress, such as the events surrounding the break-up of their parents' marriage; and (3) recovery from trauma, especially the horrors of civil wars and concentration camps. Under all three conditions, they have discerned a common core of individual dispositions and sources of support in the extended family and community that seem to transcend ethnic, geographic, and social-class boundaries.

Teachers and school were among the most frequently encountered protective factors for children in the Kauai Longitudinal Study who successfully overcame the multiple odds of poverty, perinatal stress, parental psychopathology, and family dysfunctions (Werner & Smith, 1992). From grade school through high school and community college, resilient youngsters encountered a favorite teacher who became a positive role model for them. Even among child survivors of concentration camps, a special teacher had a potent influence on their lives, provided them with warmth and caring, and taught them "to behave compassionately" (Werner, 1990).

Most longitudinal studies of resilient children have noted that they enjoy school, whether nursery school, grade school, or high school, and make it a "home away from home," a refuge from a dysfunctional household. The more successful inner-city schools tend to maintain realistically high academic standards, provide effective feedback with ample praise, and offer positions of trust and responsibility to their students. Such structural support appears to be an especially potent protective factor for children from divorce-prone homes and minority backgrounds (Werner, 1990).

Based on their readings of the research literature and their considerable "hands-on" experience in schools, Nan Henderson and Mike Milstein have presented us with a beautifully written book, *Resiliency in Schools: Making It Happen for Students and Educators,* which should be read by all administrators, teachers, and parents concerned with the future of their children. In eight concise chapters, the authors show us how caring people in an educational setting can foster resiliency in themselves, in the classroom, and among individual children. They expose us to a broad range of activities that have been tried in school and community settings and, most important, provide the reader with assessment and evaluation tools with which to monitor the process of changing schools to enhance protective factors in the lives of students and teachers.

A *word of caution* is in order: The study of resilient children has informed us about large individual differences among youngsters exposed to risk and stress. It should not come as a surprise to the reader that they will also encounter individual differences in the responses of students and educators to a wide range of intervention strategies that aim to foster resiliency. Although Henderson and Milstein offer a wide array of options that can be tried in schools and communities with "at-risk" children, most of these "change processes" seem to have been relatively short-lived and are dependent on the life cycle of grant support garnered for each project. The Resiliency Wheel that is the core of their presentation is a useful heuristic tool for assessment and intervention, but it needs to be supplemented by concrete outcome measures that show lasting positive change in the behavior of the children and teachers who participated in these intervention programs, and it should be documented by independent observers. The questions readers have to ask themselves after reading this book are succinctly summarized in the concluding chapter: "How would we know we have succeeded in resiliency building?" "What measures would we use?" "Who would we use them with?" and

"When would we use them?" The authors provide no *definite* answers to these questions in this book but challenge each of us to consider these issues in the context of our own work with students and educators.

Emmy E. Werner
Research Professor (Human Development)
University of California at Davis

References

Werner, E. E., & Smith, R. S. (1992). *Overcoming the odds: High risk children from birth to adulthood.* Ithaca: Cornell University Press.

Werner, E. E. (1990). Protective factors and individual resilience. In S. Meisel and J. Shonkoff (Eds.), *Handbook of early intervention* (pp. 97-116). Cambridge: Cambridge University Press.

About the Authors

Nan Henderson is a speaker, consultant, and author on fostering resiliency and wellness in children, youth, and adults, and on school and organization change. She teaches in the Alcohol and Drug Studies Program at the University of New Mexico and has directed districtwide, citywide, and statewide prevention and student assistance programs.

Henderson's professional career includes several years as a clinical social worker providing services to youth and their families in agencies, schools, and private practice. She is cofounder and editor-in-chief of a national journal, *Resiliency in Action*, cocreator of a video, *How Schools Are Creating Resilient Children*, and coauthor of a book, *Motivating Schools to Change: Integrating the Threads of School Restructuring*.

Mike M. Milstein is Professor of Educational Administration at the University of New Mexico. Prior to this position, he was a professor of educational administration at SUNY/Buffalo. His teaching, research, and writing interests are in the areas of resiliency, organizational change, and organizational development.

Milstein has been actively engaged in school restructuring, with a special interest in educator plateauing and resilience. He has facilitated urban school district restructuring teams; provided guidance for rural school district administrative teams; and helped many schools develop structures, modify roles, and learn the necessary skills for effective school restructuring.

For Mary Sue Iverson, to whom I owe my resiliency—
my grandmother, my role model, and a resiliency-building
public school teacher for 50 years

WITH LOVE, N. H.

For Martin Milstein, a special father and a superb
resiliency role model

M. M.

1

Resiliency Defined

*In the 1980s in this country, the Damage Model seeped
down from the professional to our popular culture in a big
way. . . . How can we escape the pessimism of the Damage
Model prediction? . . . We need to hear less about our
susceptibility to harm and more about our ability to
rebound from adversity when it comes our way.*

STEVEN AND SYBIL WOLIN (1993, p. 20)

Schools today are facing the difficult challenges of ensuring success for all students and fostering an empowered, enthusiastic staff of lifelong learners. This book is about developing "resiliency," a new paradigm of student and staff development that offers schools a coherent, research-based framework for the achievement of these goals. In this chapter, resiliency is defined, the research base for this paradigm is examined, and a six-step plan of action for resiliency building is introduced. The overall purpose of this book, making resiliency a reality for both students and educators, is also described.

Chapters 2, 3, and 4 focus on what resiliency building looks like for students, for educators, and in schools as organizations, respectively. Chapters 5 and 6 describe and offer examples of how schools can change to be better resiliency builders. Chapters 7 and 8 provide specific tools educators can use in resiliency building in their schools.

The Emergence of Resiliency

The foundation for the resiliency paradigm is a dramatic new perspective on how children and adults bounce back from stress, trauma, and risk in their lives that is emerging from the fields of psychiatry, psychology, and sociology. A growing number of studies in these fields challenge the notion that stress and risk (including abuse, loss and neglect, or simply the ordinary stresses of life) inevitably doom people to develop psychopathologies or perpetuate cycles of poverty, abuse, educational failure, or violence.

The idea of resiliency, that people can bounce back from negative life experiences and often become even stronger in the process of overcoming them, has emerged from this research. A call to action to focus on, understand, and enhance the development of resiliency is arising not only from social scientists but also from educators who are beginning to understand the need for schools to be resiliency-fostering institutions for all who work and learn in them. Resiliency studies, in fact, offer evidence of what educators have long suspected and hoped: More than any institution except the family, schools can provide the environment and conditions that foster resiliency in today's youth and tomorrow's adults. Achieving the stated goals of academic and life success for all students and an enthusiastic, motivated, change-oriented staff involves increasing student and staff resiliency.

Importance of The School

The Purpose of This Book

This book was written to assist students, teachers, administrators, and others in the school community in becoming more adept at fostering resiliency in themselves and others. An understanding of resiliency, its importance, and the ways schools can help people bounce back and evolve into more competent and successful learners, workers, and citizens, is needed now more than ever.

American culture fixates on the negative and in education, too often, the discouraged and discouraging. Schools are increasingly attacked for not producing more successful learners. School staffs respond by pointing out the increase in societal problems including drug use, divorce, crime, and violence that hamper their effectiveness. They feel a lack of community support, appreciation, and recognition coupled with increased pressure to do "more with less." This situation often contributes to an "us versus them" mentality rather than the ideal of a collaborative school community.

Fixation on The negative

The focus on the study of "risk" in students' lives and the identification of a myriad of "risk factors" have also contributed to a feeling of discouragement about children and youth. Adults have come to believe that the extensive risks in children's lives, which are indeed a reality, doom an increasing number of children to negative outcomes—dropping out of school, using drugs, going to prison.

The resiliency research, along with the theory and helping strategies emerging from it, offers a more positive and a more accurate perspective. It offers hope based on scientific evidence that many, if not most, of those who experience stress, trauma, and "risks" in their lives can bounce back. It challenges educators to focus more on *strengths instead of deficits*, to look through a lens of strength in analyzing individual behaviors, and confirms the power of those strengths as a lifeline to resiliency. It shows what is "right" in the lives of people, overlooked until recently, which can build a path of triumph over all that was "wrong." Most important, it indicates what must be in place in institutions, especially schools, for resiliency to flourish in the lives of students and adults who learn and work there.

Changing Attitudes

Resiliency research is contributing to a philosophical revolution away from a pathology-based medical model of human development to a proactive wellness-based model. The Wellness Model focuses on the emergence of competence, empowerment, and self-efficacy. Resiliency researchers criticize the "meager regard for the forces that keep people healthy" in the fields of psychology and psychiatry, noting the "comfort with identifying, categorizing, and labeling diseases" (Wolin & Wolin, 1993, p. 13)—a criticism that can also be applied to education. They call upon their colleagues to "fully explore the wellsprings of individual strength" (Higgins, 1994, p. 2). Many have embraced this new attitude about risk, stress, and trauma: With an adequate resiliency-supporting environment, strength can emerge from adversity (Higgins, 1994; Richardson, Neiger, Jensen & Kumpfer, 1990; Werner & Smith, 1992; Wolin & Wolin, 1993).

Based on her extensive reviews of the resiliency research, Benard (1991) concludes that everyone has a capacity for resiliency that should be recognized. Characteristics of resiliency can be discovered in almost everyone if they are examined for signs of resiliency with the same meticulousness used in looking for problems and deficits. The process of resiliency development is, in fact, the process of life, given that all people must overcome stress and trauma and disruption in the process of living. A resiliency-building attitude involves searching for resilience, "any scrap of it" (Higgins, 1994, p. 322), looking for the times you or your students "outmaneuvered, outlasted, outwitted, or outreached" the adversity that you encountered (Wolin & Wolin, 1993, p. 7).

Risk Research Versus Resiliency

Resiliency research differs from the decades of research on "risk" that contributed extensively to the deficit, pathology-focused model that permeates views of human development. Most risk research focuses on individuals who are already having problems such as drug abuse, school failure, and criminal involvement. Once these troubled individuals are identified, risk researchers look at their personal histories, examine their current environmental conditions, and find specific *correlates* that exist in their lives. These correlates, referred to as "risk factors," are well known by most school staff and include family addiction, poverty, neglect, negative school climate, community disorganization, and lack of access to basic human needs.

Risk research is limited, however, because it does not clearly show cause versus effect. For example, were the circumstances and characteristics of people who developed addiction or experienced school failure or became involved in criminal behavior the cause or the result of their problems? Does alcoholism lead to homelessness or does homelessness lead to alcoholism? Does a lack of social skills in a child lead to antisocial behavior or do children with antisocial tendencies have trouble integrating and using appropriate social skills?

The response to this cause-effect dilemma was a research design that is developmental and longitudinal. In this type of research, children—and occasionally young adults—are assessed at various times during the course of their development to better understand the development of disorders. With this design, "a consistent—and amazing—finding [has] emerged: Although a certain percentage of these

The initial study

high-risk children developed various problems (a percentage higher than in the normal population), a greater percentage of the children became healthy, competent young adults" (Benard, 1991, p. 2).

In contrast to retrospective studies, longitudinal studies have shown that this is the case *even among children exposed to several potent risk factors*. In short, longitudinal research has corrected an inaccurate impression left by risk research: Many, if not most, children identified as "high risk" *do not* develop the litany of problems educators have come to expect. They are from high-risk circumstances but they are "resilient." Clearly, we need "a corrective lens—an awareness of the self-righting tendencies that move children toward normal adult development under all but the most adverse circumstances" (Werner & Smith, 1992, p. 202).

The main finding of my study

Adults in the Resiliency Literature

Because almost all of the resiliency research to date has focused on children and adolescents, an understanding of how adults exposed to both personal and work-related stress bounce back is just emerging. From our own observations and from reviewing the work of researchers who are expanding their studies to include adults, it appears the process of resiliency building is similar for children and for adults. This process has been diagrammed in a Resiliency Model (Richardson et al., 1990) that is summarized in Figure 1.1.

According to the Resiliency Model, when an individual of any age experiences adversity, he or she also—ideally—experiences individual and environmental characteristics, protective factors, that buffer that adversity. With enough "protection," the individual adapts to that adversity without experiencing a significant disruption in his or her life. The individual stays within a comfort zone, or at "homeostasis," or moves to a level of increased resiliency because of the emotional strength and healthy coping mechanisms developed in the process of overcoming the adversity. Without the necessary protection, an individual goes through a process of psychological disruption, then over time reintegrates from that disruption. Again, the availability of personal and environmental protective factors will govern the type of reintegration. As shown in Figure 1.1, this reintegration may take on

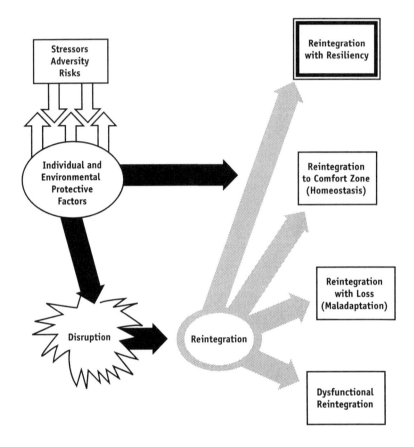

Figure 1.1. The Resiliency Model
SOURCE: Adapted from Richardson, Neiger, Jensen, & Kumpfer, 1990.

characteristics of dysfunction such as alcohol or other drug abuse or attempted suicide, or characteristics of maladaptation such as a loss of self-worth or loss of the capacity for healthy coping. Reintegration may also eventually result in an individual's return to the comfort zone or increased resiliency.

The Resiliency Model offers two important messages: that adversity does not automatically lead to dysfunction but can result in a number of outcomes for the individual experiencing it and that even an initial dysfunctional reaction to adversity can, over time, improve.

Richardson and his colleagues (1990) suggest that the process diagrammed in the Resiliency Model is applicable to every person alive because it is, indeed, the process of life.

The environment is critical to an individual's resiliency in two ways. First, the internal protective factors that assist an individual in being resilient in the face of a stressor or challenge are often the result of environmental conditions that foster the development of these characteristics. Second, immediate environmental conditions present, in addition to the stressor or challenge, contribute to shifting the balance of an individual's response from one of maladaptation or dysfunction to homeostasis or resiliency.

Resiliency and Protective Factors Defined

There is no universally accepted definition of "resiliency," although most definitions used in the literature are very similar. Richardson and his colleagues (1990) have described it as "the process of coping with disruptive, stressful, or challenging life events in a way that provides the individual with additional protective and coping skills than prior to the disruption that results from the event" (p. 34). Higgins (1994) echoes this focus in describing resiliency as the "process of self-righting and growth" (p. 1). The Wolins (1993) define resiliency as the "capacity to bounce back, to withstand hardship, and to repair yourself" (p. 5). They explain that the term "resilient" has been adopted instead of earlier terms researchers used to describe the phenomenon, such as invulnerable, invincible, and hardy, because "resilient" recognizes the pain, struggle, and suffering involved in the process.

In focusing on students and educators, the following definition adapted from Rirkin and Hoopman (1991), which contains the elements of resiliency building that should occur in schools, is useful: *Resilience can be defined as the capacity to spring back, rebound, successfully adapt in the face of adversity, and develop social, academic, and vocational competence despite exposure to severe stress or simply to the stress that is inherent in today's world.* It is clear from this definition that every student today, indeed every person young and old, needs to develop resiliency.

Resilience is a characteristic that varies from person to person and can grow or decline over time; protective factors are characteristics within the person or within the environment that mitigate the negative impact of stressful situations and conditions. Schools can embody both the environmental conditions that foster resilient reactions to immediate circumstances and the educational approaches, prevention and intervention programs, and appropriate curricula to develop individual, internal protective factors. A list of protective factors, both internal and external, is included in Table 1.1.

This awareness points to the resiliency-building solution for both academically or socially failing children and overwhelmed, change-weary, or demoralized school staff: Build in more protective factors. The goal is to shift the balance to offset the impact of stressful life events. When this balance is favorable, successful adaptation is possible. "However, when stressful life events outweigh the protective factors, even the most resilient . . . can develop problems" (Werner, 1990, p. 111).

Profile of a Resilient Person

Resilient children and resilient adults look remarkably similar. Benard (1991) characterizes *resilient children* as socially competent, with life skills such as problem solving, critical thinking, and the ability to take initiative. In addition, resilient children have a sense of purpose and foresee a positive future for themselves. They have special interests, goal directedness, and motivation to achieve in school and in life.

Higgins (1994) characterizes *resilient adults* similarly, noting their positive relationships, adept problem solving, and motivation for self-improvement. Educational motivation is also obvious in adults as evidenced by their educational attainment. They are often purposefully involved in social change and activism and typically have a sense of faith, considering themselves either spiritual or religious. Most show the ability to construe some meaning and usefulness from the stress, trauma, and tragedy they have experienced. Higgins points out, however, that many adults who consider themselves resilient report that when they were children, the seeds of their resiliency were not always obvious to themselves or to others.

TABLE 1.1 Internal and Environmental Protective Factors

Internal Protective Factors:
Individual Characteristics That Facilitate Resiliency

1. Gives of self in service to others and/or a cause
2. Uses life skills, including good decision making, assertiveness, impulse control, and problem solving
3. Sociability; ability to be a friend; ability to form positive relationships
4. Sense of humor
5. Internal locus of control
6. Autonomy; independence
7. Positive view of personal future
8. Flexibility
9. Capacity for and connection to learning
10. Self-motivation
11. Is "good at something"; personal competence
12. Feelings of self-worth and self-confidence

Environmental Protective Factors:
Characteristics of Families, Schools, Communities,
and Peer Groups That Foster Resiliency

1. Promotes close bonds
2. Values and encourages education
3. Uses high-warmth, low-criticism style of interaction
4. Sets and enforces clear boundaries (rules, norms, and laws)
5. Encourages supportive relationships with many caring others
6. Promotes sharing of responsibilities, service to others, "required helpfulness"
7. Provides access to resources for meeting basic needs of housing, employment, health care, and recreation
8. Expresses high and realistic expectations for success
9. Encourages goal setting and mastery
10. Encourages prosocial development of values (such as altruism) and life skills (such as cooperation)
11. Provides leadership, decision making, and other opportunities for meaningful participation
12. Appreciates the unique talents of each individual

SOURCE: Adapted from Richardson et al., 1990; Benard, 1991; Werner and Smith, 1992; Hawkins, Catalano, & Miller, 1992

Seven internal characteristics, termed "resiliencies," have been proposed as typical in both resilient children and adults by the Wolins (1993) based on their studies of children and youth from alcoholic and other stressful environments. The Wolins report that besides developing various levels of problems from growing up in dysfunctional environments, individuals also develop these internal resiliencies, any one of which can serve as a lifeline for the resilient overcoming of any "damage." The resiliencies are initiative, independence, insight, relationship, humor, creativity, and morality. Signs of their development vary with age.

Initiative in a young child is evidenced by the child's exploring his or her environment and in an adult by the individual's ability to take action. Independence in a young child may be seen in that child's straying or disengaging from unpleasant circumstances; an adult behaves with autonomy, the ability to separate oneself from external situations. Insight in a child is evidenced by the child sensing that something is wrong in an environmental situation; an adult shows a more developed perception of what is wrong and why it is wrong. When a young child seeks to connect with others, he or she is exhibiting relationship resiliency; an adult with this resiliency has a complex set of abilities that enable him or her to form relationships with others. Humor and creativity in adults are self-explanatory; in children both are evidenced by playing. Morality in a child is shown by that child's judgment of right and wrong; in adults morality means altruism and acting with integrity.

The Wolins (1993) state that even one of these characteristics in a child or an adult can be enough to propel that person to overcome challenges of dysfunctional and stressful environments and that additional resiliencies often develop from an initial single strength. They explain that individuals who encounter family dysfunction or other environmental stresses often react with a dual response of both negative behavior and resiliency behavior. Often behavior seen as dysfunctional (such as running away from home, for example) may in fact contain elements of resiliency (such as initiative and independence). Reframing such behavior to include its positive elements—without necessarily condoning it—can facilitate the resiliency-building process. They also recommend pointing out and complimenting resiliency behavior often.

Resiliency researchers emphasize that resiliency is a *process* more than a list of traits. Although it appears that some individuals have genetic tendencies that contribute to their resiliency, such as an outgoing, social disposition and physical attractiveness (Werner & Smith, 1992), most of the characteristics associated with resiliency can be learned (Higgins, 1994). In the following section, the environmental conditions that both help build the internal resiliency characteristics described above and provide the environmental protective factors are examined.

Six Steps to Fostering Resiliency

The risk and resiliency literature emphasizes that schools are critical environments for individuals to develop the capacity to bounce back from adversity, adapt to pressures and problems encountered, and develop the competencies—social, academic, and vocational—necessary to do well in life. Six consistent themes have emerged from this research showing how schools as well as families and communities can provide both the environmental protective factors and the conditions that foster individual protective factors. These themes form a six-step strategy for fostering resiliency in schools that is introduced here and expanded upon throughout each of the following chapters. These steps are diagrammed in Figure 1.2, the Resiliency Wheel.

Steps 1 Through 3: Mitigating Risk

Risk factor research, which encompasses hundreds of studies over several decades, has been thoroughly examined by Hawkins, Catalano, and Miller (1992), who have also conducted their own studies of risk and protection over the past 2 decades. They have concluded that the risk literature suggests three main strategies for mitigating the impact of risk in the lives of children and youth, in effect moving them toward resiliency (Hawkins & Catalano, 1990).

1. *Increase bonding.* This involves increasing the connections between individuals and any prosocial person or activity and is based

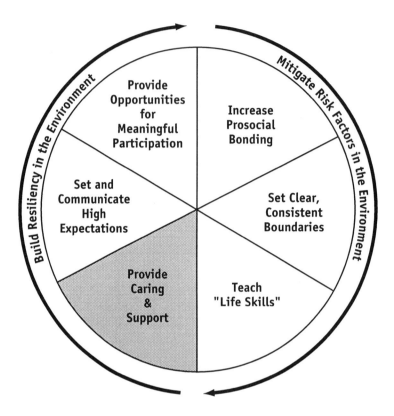

Figure 1.2. The Resiliency Wheel

on the evidence that children with strong positive bonds are far less involved in risk behaviors than children without these bonds. Similarly, school change literature also focuses on bonding students to school and academic accomplishment through connecting to each student's preferred learning style.

2. *Set clear and consistent boundaries.* This involves the development and consistent implementation of school policies and procedures and speaks to the importance of clarifying expectations of behavior. These expectations should include addressing risk behaviors for students and should be clearly written, clearly communicated, and coupled with appropriate consequences that are consistently enforced.

3. *Teach life skills.* These include cooperation, healthy conflict resolution, resistance and assertiveness skills, communication skills, problem-solving and decision-making skills, and healthy stress management. When these skills are adequately taught and reinforced, they help students successfully navigate the perils of adolescence, especially the use of tobacco, alcohol, and other drugs (Botvin & Botvin, 1992). These skills are also important in creating an environment that is conducive to students' learning and in assisting adults in being able to engage in effective interactions within the school.

Steps 4 Through 6: Building Resiliency

The resiliency research yields three additional steps that are important in fostering resiliency. Benard (1991) synthesized these findings into the following recommendations, which are environmental conditions typically present in the lives of individuals who bounce back:

4. *Provide caring and support.* This includes providing unconditional positive regard and encouragement. Because it is the most critical of all the elements that promote resiliency, it is shaded on the Resiliency Wheel. In fact, it seems almost impossible to successfully "overcome" adversity without the presence of caring. This caring does not necessarily have to come from biological family members. Often teachers, neighbors, and youth workers provide it (Werner & Smith, 1992), as well as other elements of resiliency fostering. Peers and even pets can also serve as resiliency builders for adults and children (Higgins, 1994).

Educational reformers are recognizing that caring environment is critical as the foundation for academic success. Noddings (1988) notes, "It is obvious that children will work harder and do things— even odd things like adding fractions—for people they love and trust" (p. 32).

5. *Set and communicate high expectations.* This step appears consistently in both the resiliency literature and the research on academic success. It is important that expectations be both high and *realistic* in order to be effective motivators. In reality, however, many children in schools, especially those stuck with one or more of the myriad of

labels used in schools, experience unrealistically low expectations and adopt low expectations for themselves. School staff complain that this is also true for adults in schools, whose abilities and potentials are often unrecognized or undervalued.

6. *Provide opportunities for meaningful participation.* This strategy means giving students, their families, and staff a lot of responsibility for what goes on in school, providing opportunities for problem solving, decision making, planning, goal setting, and helping others. This resiliency builder is also increasingly showing up in school change literature with expectations that teaching become more "hands-on," curriculum more "relevant" and "real world" and decision making more site-based, actively involving all members of the school community (Cooper & Henderson, 1995).

Employed in combination, these six approaches have resulted in increased positive self-concepts, attachment to school, a belief in rules, and higher standardized test scores, as well as significant decreases in delinquency, drug use, and suspensions for students (Hawkins et al., 1992). They consistently appear as critical factors in fostering resiliency in children and adults.

Using the Resiliency Wheel

The Resiliency Wheel can be used in resiliency building in individuals, groups, or entire organizations, because the necessary conditions for fostering resiliency are the same for each. Another way to view the Resiliency Wheel is as a Resiliency Web. Any person or group or organization can be assessed as to how strong the strands of the web are in each of the six quadrants, and all can benefit from weaving more strands, more protection, in every quadrant.

In the following chapters, we will show the application of the resiliency wheel to fostering resiliency in students (chapter 2), fostering resiliency in educators (chapter 3) and changing schools into more effective resiliency-building organizations (chapter 4). Chapters 5 through 8 focus on the process of changing a school into a more effective resiliency-building organization, with an emphasis on specific strategies, activities, and examples that can be used in any school.

Resiliency as a Process

One of the most hopeful findings from the resiliency literature is that resiliency building is a long-term process. A snapshot of anyone at any given time does not accurately convey the capacity within to become more resilient. Many children living in high-risk environments, for example, do not fully develop their resiliency until adulthood (Werner & Smith, 1992); most adults described in Higgins's (1994) study of resilient adults noted that they would not have qualified for the study at earlier times in their lives.

This reality can, however, also be discouraging in a culture that demands a "quick fix" approach. We do not want resiliency to be viewed as another characteristic that people either have or do not have. Rather, in the following chapters we offer specific strategies indicated by the resiliency and effective-schools research that schools can use to enhance the process of resiliency development in both students and educators.

In Conclusion

Resiliency is a characteristic critical to student and educator success. Everyone has some resiliency characteristics, though those traits often go unnoticed, and more resiliency can be developed. Schools can use the resiliency paradigm as a comprehensive model for developing academic and social success for all students and an empowered, motivated staff able to meet the challenges of education today. Resiliency development is facilitated by the six steps diagrammed in the Resiliency Wheel.

Chapter 2 describes in more detail how important schools are as resiliency-developing environments for students. Ways of developing student resiliency are outlined and real-world examples of resiliency building in schools are included.

Activities

1. Identify someone you know who fits the definition of "resilient." Ask this person about the people, circumstances, and organizations

that facilitated his or her resiliency. What personal traits does he or she identify that helps him or her to be resilient? How has this person's resiliency increased over time?

2. Examine your own resiliency. When have you bounced back? Who and what helped you in this process? What strengths do you see in yourself that have been fostered through adversity? Which of the Wolins' seven resiliencies can you identify in yourself?

3. Who and what currently provides you with the six steps to resiliency identified in this chapter? Do you need to find additional resiliency builders in your life?

4. Look over the Resiliency Wheel. Identify things you are doing in each section of the wheel to build resiliency for students. Identify ways your school as a whole builds resiliency for students. Identify ways your school and district build staff resiliency. Are there segments of the wheel that are missing or somewhat flat for students or staff, or both, in your school?

2

How Schools Foster Resiliency in Students

I probably survived because of my school teachers . . . an adult role model that was caring.

"TERRY," IN THE VIDEO *SURVIVOR'S PRIDE:*
BUILDING RESILIENCE IN YOUTH AT RISK
(WOLIN & WOLIN, 1994)

The evidence that schools as organizations and education in general can be powerful resiliency builders abounds. Next to families, schools are the most likely place for students to experience the conditions that foster resiliency. Though schools have the power of resiliency building, more can be done to ensure that it happens for all students. How schools build resiliency in students and what they must do to become more effective as resiliency builders is the focus of chapter 2. The ways resiliency is built in school, the conditions necessary for it to take place, and profiles of resiliency-building classrooms are also included in this chapter.

Relationships and Resiliency Building

Two themes that consistently appear in the effective-schools literature (Fiske, 1992) are equally applicable to student resiliency building—caring and personalization. More than any other way, schools build resiliency in students through creating an environment of caring personal *relationships*. Those relationships begin with educators who have a resiliency-building attitude, an approach that conveys hope and optimism (no matter what a student's challenges or past behavior). It's an attitude that says, "I believe you can make it, you are 'at promise' rather than 'at risk.'" Resiliency-building relationships in schools are also characterized by a focus on students' strengths. Adults in schools, in fact, need to look for student strengths with the same meticulousness that is usually used to uncover student problems, and mirror those strengths to the student. This doesn't mean ignoring behavior that is inappropriate or risky. It simply means balancing the picture so that a student receives at least as much feedback on strengths, including those described in the profile of resilient people in chapter 1, as he or she does on problems. The resiliency literature is clear: A student's strengths are what will propel him or her from "risk" behavior to resiliency.

> An enormous body of research has documented the deleteri-
> ous effects of programs that [negatively] label and track kids.
> . . . The labeling process is clearly a demotivator to change.
> For change to happen, people have to have a sense of self-
> efficacy. They have to believe and have hope that they have
> the strengths and the abilities to make positive changes.
> (Benard, 1993, p. 28)

Students internalize this belief and hope through the interactions they have with others. The most critical resiliency builder for every student is a basic trusting relationship, even with just one adult, within the family or without, that says, "You matter" (Werner, cited in Gelham, 1991).

Resiliency is also built in students by creating school environments characterized by the six resiliency-building factors introduced in chapter 1. Classrooms, school sites, and entire school districts can work on the incorporation of these six factors. In short, resiliency is built in students by one-to-one interactions that convey optimism and a strength focus and by encountering the six resiliency-building factors in the structure, teaching strategies, and programs in the school organization.

Barriers to Resiliency Building for Students

As detailed in chapter 1, for decades, educators have been guided by a risk-deficit view of students. This view promotes meticulously identifying problems, weaknesses, risks, and deficits and labeling students according to this assessment, with little effort given to identifying and building on student strengths.

The goal of risk research has been to identify student vulnerabilities so that interventions could be implemented that would mitigate the risks, thus promoting positive student outcomes in the face of these risks. *In reality, however, deficit labels on students have become self-fulfilling prophecies* for students rather than a path to resiliency. A typical, though often unspoken, attitude toward a student identified with many risks or deficits is, "This kid is doomed."

Resiliency research challenges this attitude and provides the basis for the "resiliency attitude" described above by showing scientific evidence that protective factors, many of which can be learned or provided environmentally, "make a more profound impact on the life course of children . . . than do specific risk factors or stressful life events" (Werner & Smith, 1992, p. 202).

Many educators report that they have sensed resiliency in their students. They are *just now learning the terminology* to identify it. Without knowing the specifics, however—that is, the characteristics of children who are developing resiliency even in high-risk environments—it is less likely that educators will be effective in looking for resiliency, identifying it, and helping students identify it in themselves. *Without an awareness of exactly what contributes to resiliency*, it is also more difficult to promote programmatic and structural changes that build resiliency in students.

Even with an understanding of resiliency, attitudes change slowly. Many barriers to school change, in general, also impede changing schools to foster resiliency. *Perceived time limitations* is one of these barriers, though an encouraging finding from the resiliency research is that resiliency often can be fostered with limited amounts of "clock time" (Higgins, 1994, p. 324) by using in different ways the time that is available. However, because building resiliency is about building relationships, schools that do not make time for relationship building will not be effective resiliency builders.

Evidence gathered by teachers who have shadowed students to find out what being in a particular school is really like for students supports the need to change how time is used in schools. The reaction of one high school's teachers to this experience is indicative of the lack of relationships in school that many, if not most, secondary students experience: Teachers returned from shadowing students and reported: "'Nobody spoke to me' and 'Nobody asked me a question.'

They said that school was not a very humane place. You never got to make a decision. You never got to think. Nothing was connected with anything else." (Fiske, 1992, p. 88)

Controversy over the role of school in the lives of students is another barrier to resiliency building, that is, the idea that educators should just "teach the basics." This barrier is related to the still-prevalent factory model of schooling, in which students are objects to be socialized into good employees in an industrial society (Cooper & Henderson, 1995). The reality of students' lives in the factory model of schooling, as described above by teachers shadowing students in such schools, clarifies why the factory model is a barrier not only to resiliency building but to bonding students to education as well.

The sheer size of schools is another barrier born from the factory model. It is more difficult to create climates of caring, form strong webs of relationships, and personalize student education or staff development in large schools. It is also more difficult to set and maintain high behavioral, academic, and professional standards in such schools. In large, anonymous schools, the prevalent adolescent culture too rarely connects with the power of an adult culture "representing serious adult ideas and concerns . . . a glimpse of possibilities that make [students] want to be grownups" (Meier, 1995a, p. 39). It is a lesson for educators that "the same American companies that gave birth to this old industrial model have been abandoning it" (Fiske, 1992, p. 27), decentralizing, reorganizing around teams of workers, adopting flexible work standards, and providing workers with the new skills necessary to play active roles in achieving the goals of the enterprise.

The absence of specific resiliency-fostering teaching strategies, school and classroom organization, and programs of prevention and intervention also are barriers to resiliency building. These are listed last because fostering resiliency is more about people-to-people interactions than about programs. However, programs reflect the attitudes of those who develop them. And the content and structure of programs can either incorporate or counteract the factors that foster resiliency.

Schools characterized by many of these barriers to resiliency building are more likely to have students who exhibit the profile shown in Figure 2.1. Specific strategies schools can use to overcome these barriers are explored in detail in chapters 5 and 6. Our experience

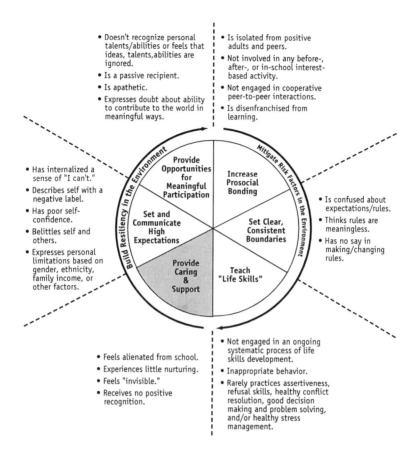

Figure 2.1. Profile of a Student Needing Resiliency Improvement

working with educators around the country over the past several decades has shown us that the greatest hope to overcoming these barriers lies in educators with attitudes that reflect the six resiliency-building factors included on the Resiliency Wheel. When an increasing number of educators convey these attitudes, appropriate programs and strategies that support resiliency building follow. This passion for helping students to be resilient, coupled with knowledge from the resiliency literature about how to do it, is the driving force behind overcoming barriers to resiliency building.

Resiliency-Building Classrooms

Many teachers manage to create resiliency-building classrooms, either through overcoming the barriers described above or because few of these barriers are in place in their schools. Resiliency-building classrooms are profiled and the actions of resiliency-building teachers in these classrooms are described below.

Profile of an Elementary School Classroom

The following profile by Duncan (1995) of a resiliency-building classroom was published in the newsletter of the Western Regional Center for Drug-Free Schools and Communities. It describes the elementary classroom of teacher Kathy Cheval, who "routinely incorporates into her teaching the protective factors that foster resiliency in kids" (p. 1).

> Some 28 children and four adults share the space. The room is filled with a quiet, subdued buzz of activity. At one table, Cheval works with a reading group; at another, a teacher's aide helps children with a language assignment. In the reading center, some children sit on the carpet at a listening center, while others share big books. Three are curled up on the couch, engrossed in their books, and two others are reading aloud to a parent volunteer. Two students work cooperatively at the computer, animatedly discussing the problems they had chosen and laughing as they succeed in solving them. Another volunteer sits in a corner surrounded by a group of children who want to practice the new vocabulary for the day. . . .
>
> The all important relationships between children are fostered in this classroom by child-developed "rights and responsibilities" [such as that everyone has the right to be safe, to be treated with kindness, to be heard, and to learn] that prohibit put-downs and affirm healthy social behavior. Problem-solving skills have been taught and practiced in role-play situations, and students are expected to use these strategies before seeking intervention from the teacher. Ap-

propriate behaviors and problem-solving skills are modeled by adults in the room, and are constantly affirmed and reinforced. As a result, children in the room treat each other with kindness and consideration, and readily volunteer to help one another. Outbursts and finger-pointing are rare occurrences. . . . The kids are also responsible for "running" the room—they set things up, clean up afterward, and inspect the clean-up. "They're tougher than I would be," Cheval says. . . .

Caring also is fostered by active involvement with younger children. Each week the children spend time with their "kindergarten buddies," reading to them and sharing their experiences. "I really love to read to my buddy," bubbles Rachel, "and she really likes it, too."

Incentives accentuate the positive. The class earns time that may be used for social activities. Sanctions emphasize logical consequences; for instance, throwing paper would result in a child spending time cleaning up the classroom.

Work expectations vary from child to child. All children are expected to do their best and are encouraged to do so, but Cheval helps where necessary. Some students receive personal assistance from a teacher or aide, some get peer tutoring, and some spend time with parent volunteers. . . .

Engagement in learning is fundamental. . . . In [this] classroom, one rarely sees teacher-centered "chalk and talk," whole-group instruction. Nearly all teacher-directed instruction occurs in small groups focused on individual abilities and needs. Much of the rest of the learning occurs in cooperative groups or with partners. On occasion, children choose to work independently. . . .

Hugs and smiles are shared in this classroom! A hug to welcome you to school, a quick "squeeze" for a job well done, a smile and nod of encouragement—all these are ways that adults and children alike show their caring.

The pervasive caring that is so evident in the classroom goes beyond its walls. Cheval has an extensive networking system set up to communicate her caring to parents. She actively enlists their help in the classroom, and keeps them busy with meaningful tasks when they are there. She sends home newsletters about the classroom activities every week, and solicits feedback from parents. When there are problems or issues to be resolved, she (and often the child involved) phones to enlist the parents' help. She also makes it a point to phone at least one parent each week to report an achievement or improvement. . . .

Appropriate behaviors are reinforced by quiet, usually private, praise. Inappropriate behaviors are dealt with by private conferences and opportunities to "try again." Rather than externally imposed discipline, problem solving is the key to conflict resolution:

- Identify the problem
- Identify the inappropriate course of action
- List options for next time
- Role-play as appropriate

"It is time consuming," Cheval says. "But by spending time at the beginning of the year, I find that the kids learn to solve conflicts in appropriate ways. In the long run, I end up spending less time intervening, and the kids develop some really important skills." (Duncan, 1995, pp. 1, 3)

Profile of a High School Classroom

The following profile of a resiliency-building secondary classroom was published in *Smart Schools, Smart Kids* (Fiske, 1992). Fiske chose the classroom because it embodied the recommendations of the effective-schools literature. Teacher Jim Streible's 11th-grade American history classroom at Fairdale High School in Louisville, Kentucky also embodies the elements of a resiliency-building environment.

There are no rows of desks. Instead students sit in clusters of four or five desks spaced around the room like satellites. One group of students is having an animated discussion about a short play they are writing about life in the 1920s and 1930s. Across the room another cluster of students is putting the final touches on a video documentary on the life of D.W. Griffith, who is buried a few miles away. . . . A third group of students is over near the lockers trying on period costumes to wear when they will dance the Charleston and show their fellow students how to do it, while a fourth group is finishing up a gigantic Hooverville house constructed from cardboard. . . . As they work, they discuss the life of the homeless of yesterday and today.

Streible keeps track of all this independent activity, unobtrusively moving from group to group, observing and listening, answering questions, prodding. . . . "I see myself as their academic coach. . . . They are the ones who do the teaching and learning. They teach themselves, and they teach each other."

Streible . . . genuinely enjoys teenagers. He listens closely to the words they use, and corrects them when a word is mispronounced. . . . While students are working in groups, he may take a student to the side of the room and talk with him or her seriously, individually. There is no room for humiliation in Streible's class. (Fiske, 1992, pp. 62, 63, 73)

Streible reports that for many years he was a traditional teacher who primarily taught by lecturing but that he now believes students must take an active role in learning—no easy task, because most students haven't ever experienced taking responsibility for their own learning. He believes this type of teaching, in which students teach themselves and one another, creates true understanding. He says that the students he now teaches are learning much better than previous classes and believes it is because they are motivated by their own interests and control over class projects.

Students agree with Streible. Their reactions convey most clearly the resiliency building that is going on in his classroom.

Jenny Abner . . . recalls her doubts at the beginning. "I was confused at first," she says. "Can this really work? What if we can't learn from each other? But you really can learn if everybody works together. . . . It makes you feel in control. You learn not only the book skills and facts but the social skills."

"The first time I got up in front of the class, I was scared to death," Bonnie [Ford] admits. . . . "I was afraid to move, and I spoke very softly so the other kids could barely hear me." She also recalls the doubts she had when Streible explained his approach. . . . "But I've really grown. This year I just get up, and it's nothing. Mr. Streible coaches us, encourages us, cheers us on. He sets up a classroom environment where we learn more, and I mean we learn it, not just memorize it. It's like a dream. . . . Now you can get up in front of class. . . . You can talk. . . . You talk about what you want to, and it makes you feel good. . . . Now I do things. I don't know if it's because of Mr. Streible's class, but I think it's a big part. Before, I'd never go to a party. Now I'm holding my own graduation party." (Fiske, 1992, p. 76)

The same adult attitudes of caring and encouragement, expressions of high and clear expectations, opportunities to learn life skills, taking charge of and participating in education (and extracurricular activities) in meaningful ways, and varied, engaging teaching strategies that bond students to school create an environment that builds resiliency in both elementary and secondary classrooms.

Applying the Six Steps of the Resiliency Wheel in Schools

The six steps to fostering resiliency detailed in chapter 1 can be expressed in both the attitudes of educators and the structure of schools. The profiles above of resiliency-building classrooms and the behavior of teachers in these classrooms document the six steps in action. The ways schools can, and have, put the six steps into practice are summarized below.

1. *Increase bonding.* Bonding is increased in schools in several ways. These include making family involvement in schooling a priority through actively recruiting parents, giving them meaningful roles in the school, offering them a variety of ways to become involved, and calling parents periodically—all parents—with some good news about their children. Setting up parent resource centers, giving parents equal say in school governance, and paying parents to build strong family involvement in schooling are also used.

Students also need a variety of in-school and before- and after-school activities. Some activities interest some students, thereby increasing their bonding, and other activities appeal to others. It is critical that arts, music, drama, sports of all kinds, community service opportunities, and clubs of all types be available (parents can be used to help provide many of these).

Teaching strategies that address multiple intelligences and multiple learning styles, as documented in the classroom profiles above, increase student bonding to learning and to staying in school.

An environment that includes each of the following steps is also one likely to increase bonding.

2. *Set clear, consistent boundaries.* This is another step that works best with the incorporation of several other resiliency-building steps. For example, it is important to involve students in the setting of these boundaries, including behavioral policy and the procedures for enforcing the policy (including consequences). An attitude of caring rather than punishment should be the foundation of these boundaries. As mentioned in chapter 1, prevention research indicates that it is important to address specific risk behaviors, such as alcohol and other drug use and violent and gang-connected behaviors, in school policy and procedures, K-12. They can be worded in ways that are developmentally appropriate.

It is also important that the staff, parents, and students all know and understand the policy. Some schools have had students draw posters reflecting the policy and mount the posters on the wall. Other schools have taken a positive, strength-building approach in writing policies, wording them in terms of student rights (to be respected, to be safe, to be drug-free, to be happy and treated with caring, etc.) that are sent home and signed by students and a family member. Examples of some of these approaches are included in chapter 7.

3. *Teach life skills.* This can be accomplished in a number of ways. A cooperative learning approach to teaching that naturally incorporates the skills for getting along, working in a group, expressing one's opinion, and goal setting and decision making is one way to teach life skills without taking a lot of extra time. Life skills can be taught as a regular course of action when students are referred to a counselor for inappropriate behavior. This is a self-efficacy-building natural consequence—students identify the skills that can help them avoid trouble

in the future, and then learn those skills. Research shows that peers are the best messengers of prevention and intervention strategies, so it is useful to identify all the ways students can help teach life skills to other students. Health curriculum is a logical place to incorporate formal life-skills training. The best life-skills training is one that offers students an adequate dosage—about 15 sessions the first year—and then booster sessions—about eight—each subsequent year (Botvin & Botvin, 1992).

4. *Provide caring and support.* As mentioned earlier, this step is the critical foundation of all resiliency building. It is the most crucial element of resiliency-building attitudes but should also be expressed by behaviors. These include noticing all students, knowing their names, drawing out the ones who may not readily participate, and investigating and intervening when students are dealing with difficult circumstances. It is expressed in allowing time in the classroom for relationship building, such as the "kindergarten buddy" program mentioned in the profile of the elementary classroom. It is also expressed in building an effective intervention model for students who are having problems and actively including strength identification and building on these student strengths in any assessment and intervention plan.

Incentive programs that offer every student a chance to succeed, like bringing a grade up one point, or getting caught and awarded on the spot or in special assemblies for "random acts of kindness," are programmatic forms of caring and support. Examples of how some schools have done this are included in chapter 7.

School staff can make a specific decision to help students find their personal resiliencies. They can listen for resiliencies and say things like "Your understanding of what is going on at home is a real strength," or "Your ability to find some laughter in your situation is an incredibly positive way of coping with what's going on," or "I'm really impressed with the way you take yourself out of that situation as a way to care for yourself and cope with it."

5. *Set and communicate high expectations.* Benard (1993) details several ways schools can implement this resiliency-building step. First, messages from school staff to students should be composed of statements such as "Think you can, work hard, get smart" and "This schoolwork I am asking you to do is important; I know you can do it; and I won't give up on you" (p. 18). Classrooms that embody high expectations are characterized by all students receiving higher-order,

more meaningful, more participatory curricula; student grouping that is heterogeneous, interest based, and flexible (with little or no tracking and labeling of students); evaluation systems that reflect the view of multiple intelligence, multiple approaches, and multiple learning styles; and lots of varying activities for all students to participate in, including community service opportunities.

Teaching strategies that communicate high expectations are cooperative rather than competitive and focus on intrinsic motivation based on interest; they also place responsibility for learning on students, through active student participation and decision making in their learning. Teachers also express high expectations by creating teacher-student relations based on individual caring for each student, taking a personalized approach to teaching, and valuing diversity.

6. *Provide opportunities for meaningful participation.* Adopting an attitude that views students as resources rather than as passive objects or problems is the critical foundation for this step. "Never do in schools what students can do" should become a motto, and each aspect of school should be analyzed for opportunities to give students more participation. This can include putting students on governance committees, even at the elementary levels (where staff have been surprised by elementary students' excellent evaluation of and suggestions for improving their school). Peer-to-peer programs, including service learning, the many before-, during-, and after-school activities available to students mentioned above, and use of participatory learning strategies are all ways of providing students with opportunities for meaningful participation.

Some schools have turned entire projects, like school-community magazines, environmental centers, and school mediation programs, over to students. Other schools have instituted leadership training for all students, including traditional and nontraditional leaders. One of the best examples of integrating this resiliency step with effective learning is a school that organized the entire fifth-grade curriculum around making and selling salsa, in which gathering and buying ingredients, cooking, bottling, marketing, distributing, and deciding how to spend the profits all were integrated.

Finding lots of parental and community business and other organization partners is important to implement effectively the six steps of resiliency building in both individual classrooms and entire schools. Our experience is that the hopeful, empowering message of

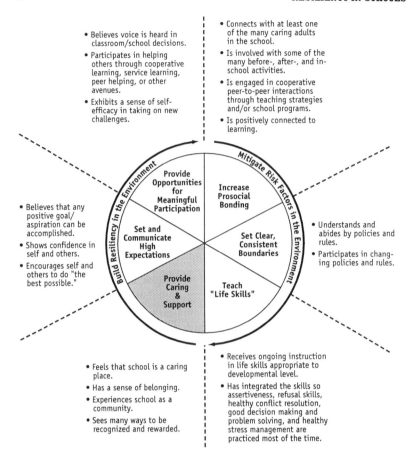

Figure 2.2. Profile of a Student With Characteristics of Resiliency

resiliency building is more successful than past approaches in cultivating the commitment from partners that is necessary.

When these six resiliency-building conditions are in place in schools so that they positively affect all students, it is more likely that students will demonstrate the profile shown in Figure 2.2.

Connecting Resiliency Building and Academic Achievement

Meier (1995b) cites research published in the *New York Times* that shows "there's a quality called 'hopefulness' that is a better predictor of success, even in college, than grade-point average, class rank, or SAT score" (p. 177) in explaining the amazing success of Central Park East in East Harlem, New York. In this high school, 90% of the students graduate and 90% of those go on to college—in a district where the average graduation rate is 50%. Challenging student curiosity, evoking a sense of wonder in learning, fostering values of democracy in the school and classroom structure, building in lots of time for respectful, caring relationships and reflection—in short, imbuing secondary education with the same spirit and ideas of the best early childhood education—has become the foundation of Central Park East (Meier, 1995b). Other profiles of "good high schools" with student academic success above the norm document these same resiliency-connected characteristics in action (Fiske, 1992; Lightfoot, 1983; Noddings, 1992).

Figure 2.3 shows the connection between each of the more programmatic and structural megatrends in education and the six resiliency-building factors. It is important to note, especially to school staff already feeling overwhelmed by too many demands, that resiliency building in students is not "one more thing." Rather, it is synonymous with the recommendations from effective-schools research as to what constitutes excellent education. It is often a relief for school staff to develop this understanding—resiliency building for students in schools is the foundation of excellent education as that concept has been defined in the last decade, and excellent education will produce resiliency building. This awareness often leads school staff to an increased buy-in to school improvement and change.

In Conclusion

Schools have the power to build academic and personal resiliency in students. Even if barriers to resiliency building for students exist in many schools, individual teachers in individual classrooms can still create havens of resiliency building—environments that are also strongly associated with academic success. Individual educators also can work to overcome the barriers to resiliency building that may exist in their larger school organizations. To do these things, however, educators themselves must be resilient; "Disempowered teachers are unlikely to create academic contexts of possibility and transformation" (Fine, 1991, p. 140). Fostering resiliency in educators is the focus of chapter 3.

Educational Change (Megatrend)   **Resiliency–Building Factors**

Educational Change (Megatrend)	Category	Resiliency–Building Factors
Develop all students into thinkers/lifelong learners	School's Purpose	High Expectations Opportunities for Meaningful Participation
Making meaning, thinking, metacognition, problem solving, using knowledge	Nature of Knowledge	Increased Bonding High Expectations Opportunities for Participation
Active learning, solving problems, using knowledge, setting own learning goals	Nature of Learning	Increased Bonding Life Skills Taught, High Expectations, Opportunities for Participation
Multidimensional teaching: guide, show, coach, intervene, provoke to action	Good Teaching	Increased Bonding Caring and Support, High Expectations, Opportunities for Participation
Based on personal learning goals, meta-cognitive, interdisciplinary, depth not breadth, project-based, connected to the real world	Curriculum	Increased Bonding Life Skills Taught, High Expectations, Opportunities for Participation
Creating leadership in others, entrepreneurial, transformational, leadership dwells in multiple roles	Leadership	Life Skills Taught, Caring and Support, High Expectations, Opportunities for Participation
Collegial, shared, involves all "stake-holders", recognizes a decision must live in hearts and minds of those who carry it out	Decision Making	Caring and Support High Expectations Opportunities for Participation
Output indicators, holistic, performance and real-world-based, learner effectiveness criteria	Assessment	Increased Bonding Caring and Support, High Expectations, Opportunities for Participation

Figure 2.3. The Connection Between Effective Education and Resiliency

Activities

1. In your mind, survey the physical environment of your classroom, office, or school building. Then, on a sheet of paper, list all the physical expressions of the six resiliency-building factors illustrated by the Resiliency Wheel that you can think of. Identify any messages in the physical environment that might be barriers to fostering resiliency in students. List some ways to change the physical environment to convey all six steps on the Resiliency Wheel.

2. Look over Figures 2.1 and 2.2. Which more accurately profiles the students in your school? Celebrate what you are doing well. Identify what you think is most important to change. Brainstorm with colleagues about how you can do it.

3. Review Figure 2.3. What are you already doing in the name of school improvement that is also building resiliency in students?

4. List 10 behaviors you already exhibit or could exhibit whenever needed to strengthen individual students' Resiliency Webs. Commit to engaging in these "random acts of resiliency building" whenever you can.

3

Resilient Students Need Resilient Educators

If we want to change the situation, we first have to change ourselves.

STEPHEN COVEY (1989, p. 18)

The need to promote resiliency among educators and ways to do so are the focus of this chapter. Factors that contribute to the lack of resiliency among educators, two profiles of resilient educators, and how the Resiliency Wheel can be used to enhance the level of resiliency among educators are explored.

Educators as Role Models

It is unrealistic to expect students to be resilient if educators are not. It is as simple as that. If educators themselves are in high-risk situations and barely coping, how can they find the energy and strength to promote resiliency among students? More important, how can students be expected to accept the challenges required to move toward resilient behaviors and attitudes if educators, some of their primary role models, do not demonstrate these qualities? If educators cannot bounce back, how can students be expected to do so?

The kinds of homes and communities from which students come are powerful contributors to the success they will have in schools. If they come from strong, supportive homes and communities, resiliency building in school may be less of an issue. If they come from homes and communities that are negative and depleting, that provide little support, bonding, or positive role models, exceptional youngsters may overcome the odds to be successful, but most will require the existence of a supportive and skillful group of educators if they are going to achieve academic and life success. It is, in fact, perhaps the only hope that many students have of moving from risk to resiliency.

Factors That Inhibit Resiliency Among Educators

As documented in chapters 1 and 2, educators are one of the critically important groups that foster student resiliency. As such, they must exhibit resiliency in themselves, but the conditions under which they work can make this difficult. The resources required to meet expectations placed on educators are in short supply. Understanding these realities, empathizing with the extraordinary challenges that educators face, and consciously striving to promote increased resiliency among this important group of professionals is crucial. Both external environmental factors and school-based factors impinge upon educator resiliency.

Environmental Factors

Educators' sense of well-being and effectiveness are challenged by three environmental factors. First, *expectations are changing about what schools should do as well as how they should do it*. Shifts toward a global economy and rapidly increasing uses of technology have placed increased demands on schools to be more creative, innovative, and responsive. In most instances, however, these expectations have not been accompanied by suggestions and training for instructional and curricular changes to meet them. Nor are they usually accompanied by increased resources.

Second, *the composition of the student population is changing*. The public school system was initially created to educate the country's youth through an elementary education level. That mandate has since been expanded to encompass secondary education. For a long period, secondary education was limited in scope, encompassing mainly students who were motivated and encouraged at home and in their communities. More recently, schools have been called upon to provide all students with a high school education.

"All students" today means something quite different from what "all students" meant in the past. Today's students come from extremely diverse socioeconomic backgrounds and national origins. The composition of the student body in most schools today is radically different and more challenging to educators than at any time in the past. Unfortunately, educators' initial professional preparation and continuing professional development usually do not place them in a confident and skillful position to cope with this challenge.

Third, whereas in the past most communities were highly supportive of their schools, currently an ever-increasing crescendo of *negative community-based criticism* is being aimed at schools. The criticism has been especially loud since the early 1980s and the publication of the report, *A Nation at Risk* (National Commission on Excellence in Education, 1983), and similar negative commentaries (Boyer, 1983; Goodlad, 1983). State legislators and governors also take critical aim at public school systems. Local communities, following suit, display disdain for the efforts and outcomes of their schools. Reputational polls regarding different occupations continually rank educators low. More telling, educators usually rank themselves even lower than does the general population.

Internal Factors

In addition to a rapidly changing set of environmental factors, school-related factors impinge on educator resiliency. First, as a group, *the educator workforce is significantly older than in the past*. During the 1960s, with other career options available, many neophyte educators made the choice to leave education after a few years in the system. Others chose to move in and out of education depending upon their family situations. Today, most school staffs are characterized by professional longevity.

Second, *many veteran educators have not opted for extensive role changes*. They remain in the same role and even the same school for their entire careers. The combination of a long time in the profession and a long time in a set role can lead to a perception of being *plateaued* (Bardwick, 1986; Milstein, 1990), which can be a detriment to resiliency. Plateauing, the sense that things have become routine, boring, or too predictable, can be a springboard toward increased resiliency *if* strategies are identified and pursued to change the situation. However, if one remains plateaued for a long period of time and is unable to overcome this state, it can become a barrier to resiliency. Research on plateauing in general and among educators specifically indicates that most people learn their jobs within 3 to 5 years. If they remain in these positions for a longer period of time, they often experience a loss of challenge, which can result in a lack of motivation, reduced enthusiasm, and increased stagnation.

Third, *structural constraints within the system* also limit individual and organizational efforts to build resiliency. These include a reward system that is tied to degrees and time in place rather than individual effort, and policies and rules that can be frustrating and debilitating (e.g., complex purchase order request procedures, limitations on personal use of school telephones, and inadequate or unclear discipline procedures). This is often compounded by an organizational culture that is reactive rather than proactive, status quo-oriented rather than change and growth-oriented (Willower, 1965).

Fourth, the environmental changes noted above have led to a *major impetus to reform the schools.* Currently termed "restructuring," this impetus has resulted in efforts to shift control from the central office to the school building (Milstein, 1993). This movement toward site-based management has challenged administrators and teachers, who must now find ways and skills for sharing power with each other, with students and their families, and with the communities they represent. These new roles focus on governance, power, decision making, assessment, and cooperation, all of which require behavioral and attitudinal changes as well as skill development on the part of everyone involved. In the long run, this will likely be beneficial for the enhancement of educator resiliency and abilities to support the resiliency building of students. For now, however, it is creating a major challenge for highly senior educator groups. Some are rising to the challenge, but others are in a bunker-mentality survival mode, or are looking for options to leave the situation.

Improving Educator Resiliency

Given these conditions, it is understandable that many educators need more resiliency development, typified by the profile shown in Figure 3.1.

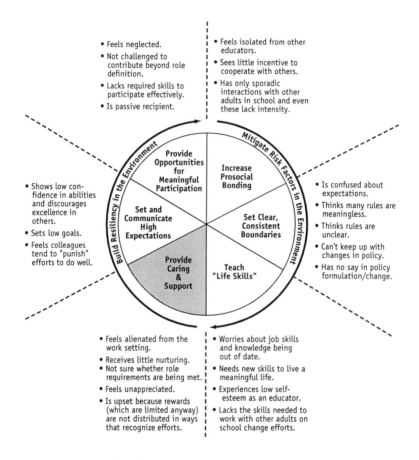

- Feels neglected.
- Not challenged to contribute beyond role definition.
- Lacks required skills to participate effectively.
- Is passive recipient.

- Feels isolated from other educators.
- Sees little incentive to cooperate with others.
- Has only sporadic interactions with other adults in school and even these lack intensity.

- Shows low confidence in abilities and discourages excellence in others.
- Sets low goals.
- Feels colleagues tend to "punish" efforts to do well.

- Is confused about expectations.
- Thinks many rules are meaningless.
- Thinks rules are unclear.
- Can't keep up with changes in policy.
- Has no say in policy formulation/change.

Mitigate Risk Factors in the Environment

Build Resiliency in the Environment

Provide Opportunities for Meaningful Participation

Increase Prosocial Bonding

Set and Communicate High Expectations

Set Clear, Consistent Boundaries

Provide Caring & Support

Teach "Life Skills"

- Feels alienated from the work setting.
- Receives little nurturing.
- Not sure whether role requirements are being met.
- Feels unappreciated.
- Is upset because rewards (which are limited anyway) are not distributed in ways that recognize efforts.

- Worries about job skills and knowledge being out of date.
- Needs new skills to live a meaningful life.
- Experiences low self-esteem as an educator.
- Lacks the skills needed to work with other adults on school change efforts.

Figure 3.1. Profile of an Educator Needing Resiliency Improvement

What does a resilient educator look like? Each individual is unique and will, therefore, have a unique profile. The basic elements of resiliency, however, will be integrated into their unique personalities. Two resilient educators, a teacher and an administrator, composites of individuals we know, are profiled below.

A RESILIENT TEACHER

Sam Harrison has taught third grade for 14 years. Over that time he has found ways to grow and stay enthused and challenged about being a teacher. During the early years of his career, he received lots of support from his principal, who also helped him to understand the "dos and don'ts" of being a good teacher. He was accepted by the veteran teachers and formed particularly close bonds with others who were relatively new to the school. Both groups encouraged him to develop his own unique classroom persona. As he learned his role, he earned the respect and admiration of his peers and his superiors. During his first 8 years as a teacher, he volunteered to participate in schoolwide decision making, including being a member of the school's curriculum committee and serving as a teacher representative to the parent-teacher association. He also pursued professional development opportunities, including achieving a master's degree in elementary education.

During the past 6 years, he has been reprioritizing his professional role at the school. He began complaining about being spread too thin and being drawn away from his primary passion—teaching children—by the many schoolwide roles he took on. Rather than become cynical and negative, he made the decision to reprioritize his efforts by reducing his schoolwide participation and focusing more intensively on his classroom responsibilities. Fortunately, his principal understood and supported this need and encouraged him to pursue his objectives. Soon after, Sam began to spend more time experimenting instructionally, introducing new or modified units in his third grade classroom and sharing his experiences with others on the faculty who showed an interest. He also began to volunteer to teach at other grade levels when the need or challenge arose. Most recently, he has been expanding his focus on his students' lives (e.g., doing more home visits and following students after they leave his classroom and even the school). With encouragement from his principal, who has given Sam increasing freedom to set his own classroom agenda, he has also begun to mentor new teachers and has volunteered to provide demonstration teaching during professional development sessions. Not surprisingly, Sam is well liked by his colleagues and has, on several occasions, been identified as the school's most outstanding teacher.

A RESILIENT ADMINISTRATOR

Maria Sanchez has been an educator for 26 years. She served as a teacher in two different middle schools during her first 6 years. By the end of that time, she began to feel a sense of boredom and routine setting in and started to think about leaving education. She decided instead to give teaching one more try. In an effort to learn new skills and challenge herself, she moved on to teach at the high school level, where she became a department chair after only 3 years. Her early experiences as chair piqued her curiosity about further opportunities to participate at a leadership level. Despite being a single parent responsible for the care of three children, she managed to prepare for the challenge of increased leadership by slowly working on and completing a master's degree in educational administration. Soon after, she was awarded a principalship at the middle school where she initially taught. Many of her early colleagues who were still at the school remembered her as a teacher and watched her closely as she assumed leadership. Ultimately, she was able to win them over. In fact, teachers have reported that she communicates clearly that she expects all students to be successful and she believes the staff is up to the challenge. They also believe that she models these expectations in her own professional behaviors. Most important, they report that they are treated with respect, care, and support, that is, as competent professionals.

Sam and Maria may appear to be quite different, but in reality they both exhibit, in their own ways, the same basic resiliency factors—the desire and capacity for bonding; defining clear boundaries; developing and exhibiting life skills; seeking and communicating caring, support, and high expectations; and capitalizing on opportunities for meaningful participation. Sam and Maria provide examples of how educators can find ways of remaining resilient over time.

Educators and the Six Resiliency-Building Factors

The six resiliency-building factors identified in Chapter 1 and applied to students in Chapter 2 are equally applicable to educators:

1. *Increase bonding.* Often educators' professional lives are spent almost exclusively in the company of their students, without regular opportunities to interact with their peers. Evaluations of teachers' and administrators' professional contributions are also frequently based on their individual classroom efforts, with only few, if any,

rewards given for teaming or other cooperative activities that promote bonding. Though the education process is often typified by
activities that are conducted in isolation from other adults, bonding
can be encouraged in several ways. First, the workday structure can
be reviewed and changed in ways that promote more opportunities
for meaningful interaction. For example, when teaming for instructional purposes is pursued, caring relations and a sense of belonging
among educators are promoted while cooperative education for students is modeled. Second, efforts to involve staff members in identifying a meaningful vision and mission can establish a feeling of
belonging to something bigger than oneself while enhancing the
potential for effective education programs. It also can break down the
artificial barriers that tend to exist between teachers and administrators as both groups understand the interconnectedness of their roles
in achieving educational excellence. Third, one-on-one interactions
such as mentoring arrangements and small-team efforts can improve
educators' sense of belonging while enriching instructional effectiveness. These strategies—cooperative professional efforts, developing
clear organizationwide purposes, and one-on-one activities—can do
much to increase bonding among educators.

2. *Set clear and consistent boundaries.* Educators conduct their activities within a complex system of "rules" (e.g., reporting and de-
parting times, service expectations, student discipline expectations,
procedures for faculty absences or for ordering materials and equipment) that often are unclear. Freedom, creativity, and growth—admi-
rable goals—are often associated with few or no constraints. In reality,
creativity and growth are possible only with expectations that are not
arbitrary, capricious, differentially applied, or, worse still, absent.
Educators will feel secure when they are clear about the boundaries
in which they exist.

Norms, rules, and policies need to be communicated clearly, and
changes that occur in them need to be shared regularly and in writing.
If educators are involved in establishing and interpreting the boundaries, they will more likely buy in to them and accept them as reason-
able and manageable. Regular reviews are important to be sure that
rules and policies are understood and appropriate.

3. *Teach life skills.* Educators need professional development to
meet the changing and growing challenges that confront them. Pre-
service preparation, at best, provides the minimum of knowledge and

skills to launch a teaching or administrative career. The rapid rate of new knowledge development, technological breakthroughs, and societal shifts and changes soon makes even this minimal modicum of preparatory knowledge and skills obsolete.

How can this situation be improved? To begin, schools can provide meaningful professional development opportunities. This requires that teachers and administrators identify their most pressing professional development needs rather than having central office personnel identify purposes and delivery formats. It also requires committing district resources for this purpose. Further, the narrow definition of professional development, which typically has to do with role improvement, can be broadened to encompass interactive processes such as goal setting, conflict management, communication, and problem solving—basic coping skills that contribute to greater resiliency. Efforts also can be made to build educator self-worth. This can be done by celebrating educators' risk taking and successes, as well as by providing adult learning opportunities focused on avocational enrichment and spiritual well-being, and promoting greater community support for educators' efforts through more effective public relations.

4. *Provide caring and support.* As professionals, educators get their most important rewards from the intrinsic satisfaction of knowing that they are performing an important function. They need to get feedback, from supervisors and peers, that communicates that they are doing their jobs well—or they may interpret the silence as an indicator of failure.

Efforts to provide such feedback are especially important because of the way extrinsic rewards (which are quite limited to begin with) are distributed. Lockstep salary systems and the relative absence of funds for special recognition purposes do not promote meaningful extrinsic rewards for individual efforts.

The sense of caring and support that is vital to educators can be enhanced in numerous ways. Informal, frequent, consistent, and reality-based messages of appreciation for positive and effective contributions, varying from brief notes to organized celebratory events, can be helpful. Leaders need to recognize how important observation and support are to those they supervise and make every effort to provide this feedback in clear and meaningful ways. In addition, positive feedback from the community and support and appreciation between colleagues need to be encouraged.

Formally changing the established reward system is important. For example, professional challenges can be introduced and differential rewards can be provided for those who accept these challenges. Implementation of reward systems that recognize outstanding contributions, or a move away from the lockstep salary system to one that provides differential rewards based upon documented differences in effort and effect, can be tried. These suggestions may be politically sensitive, but this is likely to be true of anything significant that is attempted. Rewarding extraordinary efforts and causing others to take more initiative or lose their favored position may be exactly what is required.

5. *Set and communicate high expectations.* Messages sent to educators that imply that their primary task is to maintain order and that they are expected only to make it to the end of the year with minimal disruptions suppress both educational excellence and resiliency building. If achievers are viewed as "rate busters" rather than applauded by their colleagues for going beyond minimal requirements, high expectations and excellence suffer.

How can high expectations be promoted? Most important, educators are motivated when they believe that they serve causes that are larger than themselves or their particular roles. This happens when they share a common mission as a school staff, as well as goals that can actualize the mission. It also happens through increased understanding, empathy, and appreciation of one anothers' specific contributions to making the mission and goals a reality. In practice, this means teaming, job sharing, promoting diversified roles, and encouraging individuals to make contributions that cross over particular roles. It also means keeping requirements that are not directly job related (e.g., filling out nonessential report forms) to an absolute minimum so educators can focus on performing their specific role obligations. If the work is relevant, whether related to the individual's specific role or to the overall effectiveness of the school, it needs to be protected. High expectations require that educators be given maximum time on task—that is, time to perform activities that are directly related to educational outcomes for students.

6. *Provide opportunities for meaningful participation.* Most educators have more to offer their schools than what is defined within their specific roles. Resiliency is fostered when they are given opportunities to offer their skills and energies to their work sites (e.g., a kindergarten teacher also may be an accomplished musician or a school

principal may be a skilled storyteller). As adult learners, educators need opportunities to learn new skills and participate in challenging activities.

The current emphasis on restructuring and site-based management can provide educators with meaningful roles within the larger school organization. To capitalize on this potential, several things should be considered. First, roles can be defined more broadly to include organizationwide responsibilities as well as classroom-based responsibilities for teachers. Administrators can function as facilitators of organizationwide processes as well as authoritative role players. Second, time for adults to plan together and the skills required to be able to use the time effectively can be provided. Third, focused efforts can be made to ensure that planning time leads to long-term payoffs such as a more meaningful curriculum or a clearer and more effective discipline policy, which motivates everyone to continue to participate. Finally, though encouraging schoolwide involvement is important, time to focus on primary role responsibilities must be maintained or participants will feel so diverted that they, quite appropriately, will resist future participation.

Resilient Educators

The factors explored in this chapter can foster resilient educators, profiled in Figure 3.2, which provides a sharp contrast to the imagery of Figure 3.1.

In Conclusion

Individual effort is only part of the resiliency-building process. The resiliency research clearly states that supportive environments are also necessary. What can be done to reach educators and students who do not demonstrate resiliency? What can be done to increase the likelihood of long-term, institutionalized changes that support resiliency? Achieving these goals usually requires changing the organization. Creating schools that are resiliency-building organizations for everyone who works and learns in them is the subject of chapter 4.

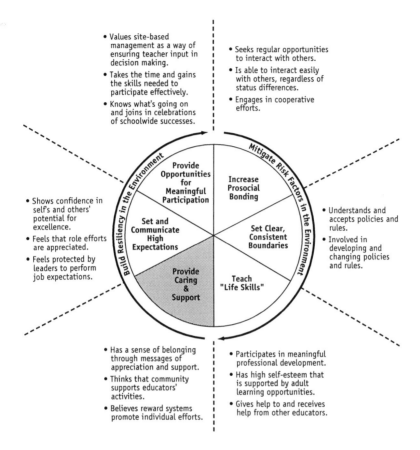

Figure 3.2. Profile of an Educator With Characteristics of Resiliency

Activities

1. Reread the brief descriptions of the two resilient educators, Sam and Maria. Identify the ways they exhibit the six resiliency-building factors described in the chapter.

2. Review Figures 3.1 and 3.2. Which describes you? In what ways? What specific activities or commitments might you need to pursue to improve your resiliency?

3. Help your colleagues identify their areas of resiliency. What has contributed to their resiliency? Why are some less resilient? Why

are some more resilient? Are there things you can identify that will increase resiliency among members of your group?

4. Read about plateauing. A good source is J. Bardwick, *Plateauing* (New York: Amacom, 1986). Are you plateaued? If so, Bardwick offers suggestions for improving your situation.

4

Characteristics of
Resiliency-Building Schools

*Loving and caring relationships should be far more valued
in schools, since it is difficult to learn anything at all
without enough love in your life. . . . Because school is the
only probable source [of resiliency] for many . . . we need
to ensure the availability of caring there.*

GINA O'CONNELL HIGGINS (1994, p. 330)

Creating and maintaining schools that organizationally promote
resiliency among the adults who work in them and the students
who study in them is the focus of chapter 4. The importance of
developing resiliency-building schools and the challenges of creating
them are reviewed. Two resiliency-building schools are profiled and
the application of the Resiliency Wheel to schools is explored.

Resilient Students and Educators
Need Resiliency-Building Schools

As discussed in previous chapters, students and educators need
to function in environments that support the development and maintenance of resiliency. Environments can hinder resiliency building in
several ways. They may be physically dilapidated and resource-poor.
They may convey little sense of purpose, direction, or the possibility
of better future states. They may send negative messages about the
worth of the people who inhabit them or may simply cause the people
in them to feel ignored. In such environmental realities, over time

even the most positive individuals may be sorely challenged and worn down.

Resiliency-building school environments can, however, be found in all types of communities. Many schools in lower socioeconomic or depressed community environments, such as Central Park East, described in chapter 2, have succeeded in providing resiliency-building settings in which students and educators alike feel cared for, safe, valued, and challenged. Similarly, many community-based organizations in lower socioeconomic communities are making strikingly positive differences in the lives of young people (McLaughlin, Irby, & Langman, 1994). On the other hand, some schools in upper socio-economic, resource-rich communities do not provide the support necessary for resiliency building among students and educators. Although the task may be more daunting when fewer resources are available, *all* schools can be designed, developed, and maintained in ways that promote resiliency.

Factors That Inhibit the
Development of Resiliency-Building Schools

Factors identified in chapter 3 that inhibit educator resiliency are also relevant to schools—changing expectations, a global economy, changing student populations, less supportive communities, an older educator workforce (many of whom remain in narrow roles over lengthy time periods), reward systems that depress rather than encourage motivation and risk taking, and the lack of knowledge and skills to engage in effective reform.

The last point—the lack of knowledge and skills required to improve schools so they can be more effective resiliency builders—is addressed in this chapter.

The rapidly changing global society and economy require a very different worker and citizen than the schools are now graduating. Indeed, the existing system is unable to prepare the graduates our country needs. The high percentage of dropouts, the large number of failing students hidden behind the mean scores on standardized tests, and the graduates who are not ready for work or additional learning constitute an embarrassing testimony. Many students leave school without even minimal skills. (*National LEADership Network*, 1991, p. 7)

In the past 20 years, much has been discovered about developing schools that promote effectiveness and resiliency. Why are such schools not emerging in greater numbers?

At a gut level all of us know that much more goes into the process of keeping a large organization vital and responsive than the policy statements, new strategies, plans, budgets, and organization charts can possibly depict. But all too often we behave as though we don't know it. If we want change, we fiddle with the strategy. Or we change the structure. Perhaps the time has come to change our ways. (Peters & Waterman, 1982, p. 3)

Most educators would agree with Peters and Waterman. Why, then, is it so difficult to rise to the challenge of changing schools? Perhaps because it requires admitting that things must be done differently, summoning the energy to do so, and taking the risks necessary to change. This is especially hard to do when the dominant culture of schools—the deeply embedded belief system about "how things should be"—is more reactive than proactive. With a primary focus on discipline, minimally acceptable outputs are emphasized. The rules and policies in this kind of culture emphasize compliance rather than risk taking. They also reward individual achievement rather than cooperation and teamwork, uniformity and predictability rather than change and diversity.

Organizational change is difficult under the best of conditions, but changing organizations characterized by the descriptions above is especially complicated. Three issues in particular affect the ability to change schools (Milstein, 1993).

1. *Change means loss and destabilization.* Individuals must first let go of something before they can move on to something else. But it is frightening to have to question beliefs and behaviors and to postpone

making final decisions. The free-floating state that accompanies change, with few if any substantial handles to hold onto during the duration—usually much longer than initially anticipated—is uncomfortable. Gaining the knowledge and skills that will be required to be effective in a targeted future state is also a challenge. Leaders often are impatient with the time the process takes and tend to view those who move slower as "resistant," which may not be the case at all. They may simply require a bit more time to come to terms with the loss of the practices they have to leave behind.

2. *Change is confusing.* Typically it is easier to agree on what is wrong than to agree on what to do to "fix" it. If a clear picture existed of where the school staff wants to be and how to get there, the staff would probably be there now. Clarity comes about only through experimentation, learning through "failures," long-term commitment, and assessment of outcomes. Most people prefer knowing where they are headed, but this is rarely possible when they take on something as significant and complex as reconceptualizing how schools are to be organized and managed.

3. *Change upsets power relationships.* Some people resist changes, even those they believe to be relevant, because they think such changes may affect detrimentally their ability to influence or control aspects of organizational life. Others may support changes that they do not wholeheartedly agree with because they think they may gain influence if such changes are instituted. In either case, behaviors may be dictated for reasons other than those related to the proposed change.

Primarily because of these factors, schools are noted for their remarkable tenacity in fending off most reform efforts. For example, during the 1960s and 1970s, when the federal government attempted to change public education through a number of fiscal incentives, many innovations were attempted, relatively few were successfully implemented, and only a handful achieved the goal of full institutionalization (Berman & McLaughlin, 1977).

Schools confronted with the inhibiting factors discussed often are unsuccessful in making necessary changes. If they are unable or unwilling to do so, they will likely exhibit few resiliency-building attributes. Figure 4.1 profiles the attributes of low-resiliency-building schools.

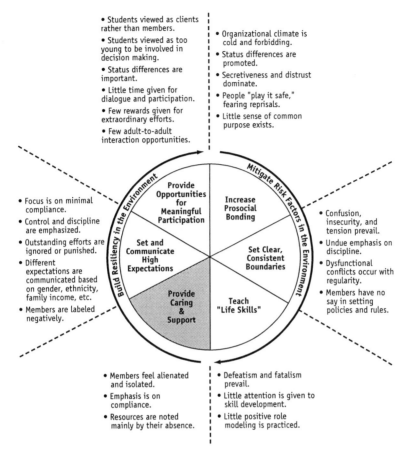

- Students viewed as clients rather than members.
- Students viewed as too young to be involved in decision making.
- Status differences are important.
- Little time given for dialogue and participation.
- Few rewards given for extraordinary efforts.
- Few adult-to-adult interaction opportunities.

- Organizational climate is cold and forbidding.
- Status differences are promoted.
- Secretiveness and distrust dominate.
- People "play it safe," fearing reprisals.
- Little sense of common purpose exists.

- Focus is on minimal compliance.
- Control and discipline are emphasized.
- Outstanding efforts are ignored or punished.
- Different expectations are communicated based on gender, ethnicity, family income, etc.
- Members are labeled negatively.

- Confusion, insecurity, and tension prevail.
- Undue emphasis on discipline.
- Dysfunctional conflicts occur with regularity.
- Members have no say in setting policies and rules.

Mitigate Risk Factors in the Environment

Build Resiliency in the Environment

Provide Opportunities for Meaningful Participation

Increase Prosocial Bonding

Set and Communicate High Expectations

Set Clear, Consistent Boundaries

Provide Caring & Support

Teach "Life Skills"

- Members feel alienated and isolated.
- Emphasis is on compliance.
- Resources are noted mainly by their absence.

- Defeatism and fatalism prevail.
- Little attention is given to skill development.
- Little positive role modeling is practiced.

Figure 4.1. Profile of a School Needing to Improve Resiliency Building

Profiles of Resiliency-Building Schools

What do resiliency-building schools look like? Two vignettes of such schools, composites of several actual settings we have worked in, provide a glimpse of what such schools look like.

Hay Elementary School

Despite the fact that the school's city-edge environment can be described as lower socioeconomic, children are performing academically beyond expectations. Much effort goes into positive partnering with the community. For example, there is an active and well-attended PTA and the school has established a secure space for community members to store necessary equipment as they do volunteer work with children. Community members, teachers, and administrators work together cooperatively on the school's site-based management team, which has developed a mission statement and operational goals to guide instructional and curricular improvement. Resources have been set aside for skill development so that everyone involved can participate effectively, with confidence and enthusiasm. Students and educators know what they are expected to do. Teachers, often with extensive student input, spend much time developing materials and activities that promote student challenges and successes. The support staff also gets into the spirit of things and encourages student achievement. It is not unusual for Hay graduates who have moved up to the middle school to return for after-school visits because they feel so much pride in the school and want to remain a part of it as long as they can. When problems and misunderstandings arise, they are confronted directly by those involved and are usually resolved to almost everyone's satisfaction. It is also important to note that the student turnover rate is lower than in comparable neighborhoods.

North High School

North High has reframed what was previously perceived as a negative situation into a positive one by recognizing the advantages of having a student body that is extremely diverse, ethnically and socioeconomically. The student body includes recent immigrants as well as longtime local residents. A focus has been placed on tolerance, acceptance, and belonging, thus making all students feel important. The school's diverse student group has come to feel at home at the school in an environment of clearly stated rules that students and staff contributed to developing and now accept. The school works closely with local businesses, tapping into their ideas and resources to enrich students' education, while ensuring this community group a constant source of skilled employees. The school provides life options from which students can choose. For example, work-study programs emphasize cutting-edge skill development. Students earn the right to participate in them by getting good grades, staying out of trouble, and receiving positive recommendations from their teachers. College-prep curricula that attract participation across the student spectrum are also in place. Teachers identify closely with the school's mission and goals and, not surprisingly, tend to remain at the school for most, even all, of their careers.

Besides serving different educational levels, Hay Elementary and North High School serve very different groups of students and communities. What they have in common, however, is an abiding faith in the importance of promoting resiliency. Both schools exhibit all six of the resiliency-promoting factors—bonding, clear boundaries, life skills training, caring and support, high expectations, and opportunities for meaningful participation.

Schools and the Six Resiliency-Building Factors

The six resiliency-building factors as they relate to students and educators have been discussed in earlier chapters. Now the focus is on schools, important crucibles within which student and educator resiliency is either nurtured or thwarted.

1. *Increase bonding.* Healthy bonding is promoted in positive, supportive organizations. Organizations have distinct climates that can be felt, much like the weather. Those who have worked in different schools know that it does not take long to feel these differences. Organizational climates can vary widely, from cold and foreboding to warm and sunny. At a deeper level, organizations also have cultures, or strongly held belief systems, that are grounded in history, tradition, and values. An organization's culture is less obvious than its climate, but it forms the foundations of how things are done at the school. At one extreme are cultures that promote status differentials and secrets and sow seeds of distrust, depress efforts to work cooperatively in teams, and send messages that emphasize the need to play it safe or risk reprisals. At the other extreme are cultures that promote equity among members, encourage risk taking and learning, and celebrate members' accomplishments because of the belief that individual achievements reflect positively on the organization.

Shaping school climate and culture is an important means of promoting resiliency. Organizational climate, like the weather, is changeable and thus easier to affect in a shorter time. Modeling preferred behaviors and encouraging a positive climate characterized by respect, trust, growth, cohesiveness, caring, support, and challenge are important ways that leaders and other members of the school community can enhance organizational resiliency building. To promote resiliency through the school's culture, school staff, students, and their families need to articulate a vision or mission, promote shared values, emphasize aspects of the school's history that are consonant with the vision or mission, and develop rituals and ceremonies that celebrate desired behaviors (Deal, 1987).

2. *Set clear and consistent boundaries.* A school can be characterized either by clear organizationally defined boundaries that promote cooperation, support, and a sense of belonging to something bigger than oneself or by confusion, uncertainty, and the tension that results. Students with unclear boundaries are likely to put undue emphasis on peer-created norms and behaviors rather than those fostered by the school. Educators, as adults, have a firmer basis upon which to make judgments about appropriate behavior, but without clear boundaries, individual objectives will likely override schoolwide objectives. Clearly stated organizational boundaries help members know when they are conducting themselves in unacceptable, minimally acceptable, or exemplary ways. As noted earlier, schoolwide efforts to explore and clarify visions, missions, and goals can provide members with a clearer and more commonly understood sense of corporate purpose. Beyond this, purposeful selection of staff, based upon their agreement with missions and goals, and the continuing professional development of this group can promote similar expectations and a sense of common destiny. Similarly, if they are to have the security of knowing what is expected of them, students need clearly stated, regularly communicated, and widely supported expectations for academic and social behavior. To increase their understanding and acceptance of these expectations, they should be involved in clarifying and defining them.

3. *Teach life skills.* Whether a school changes in ways that enhance educational effectiveness, focuses on maintenance, or slides backward sets an important example for those who work and learn within it. Does the school make efforts to improve? Does it do so effectively? Does the school support risk taking leading to individual and group skill development, or does it promote defeatism and fatalism? Mem-

bers of school organizations watch closely for signals and tend to pattern their own behaviors based on what they observe.

Resiliency-building schools promote the connection between schoolwide and individually based learning, change, and effectiveness. They monitor their environments and respond to challenges positively and with creativity. In the process, they offer members of the school community the skill development—such as critical thinking and effective problem solving—necessary to meet challenges. They also encourage cooperative behaviors such as team efforts, consensus decision making, and shared goal setting, which are life skills that transcend the classroom and the school. In these ways, schools not only promote learning but also provide positive role modeling and reward members' risk taking and growth efforts. (Milstein, 1993).

4. *Provide caring and support.* Schools can be places where people feel a sense of belonging or places that are alienating and isolating. Does the school emphasize instruction in relatively short time blocks or does it promote experimentation with other formats? Are daily routines regimented or flexible? Is the emphasis on compliance and minimally acceptable behavior or on growth and motivation? To what extent are resources—funds, materials, and equipment—gathered and made available to promote learning, growth, and well-being?

Caring and support can be promoted in schools, for all members of the school community, in several ways. First, the school can emphasize cooperation and caring, celebrations and rites of passage, and can encourage reaching out to get and give help when needed. Second, leaders can make efforts to be a presence in the school—"manage by wandering around" (Peters & Waterman, 1982)—getting to know students' names and interests, personally reaching out to families, and responding to teachers' concerns. Third, creative efforts can secure necessary human, fiscal, and material resources, which must be distributed in a fair and equitable manner for students and educators to have faith in the school's concern for their well-being and success.

5. *Set and communicate high expectations.* Schools can be places that help students and educators know that they are capable and that it matters that they do well, particularly if they have not yet internalized high expectations for themselves. Too often, however, schools send messages to both educators and students that promote minimal

compliance rather than risk taking and achievement. For students these messages include being counseled to seek entry-level jobs rather than consider further education, the acceptance of less-than-adequate academic performance, and an emphasis on control and discipline rather than challenge and opportunity. For educators they take such forms as lockstep salary schedules that do not reward individual efforts, professional development initiatives that are planned without their input or self-identified needs being taken into consideration, and lack of administrator interest, support, or involvement in their classroom activities.

How can schools be made more aware of the need to encourage high expectations? Basically, a "can do" attitude must permeate the school. Communal beliefs in the ability to succeed can be promoted and communicated with everyone encouraged to participate in the effort. In this process, educators and students will improve their self-images and will be more willing to take the risks necessary for success.

Specific strategies include a) encouraging *all* organizational members to develop growth plans—academic expectations for students and professional priorities for staff—that include clear outcome expectations; b) establishing regular review procedures and providing opportunities for supportive and corrective feedback; c) facilitating cooperative learning opportunities that encourage giving and receiving help; d) celebrating achievements; e) telling stories that emphasize effort and success; and f) developing supportive partnerships with the community.

6. *Provide opportunities for meaningful participation.* The advent of site-based management has resulted in more concern about empowering organizational members. In many schools, however, there is still a relative absence of meaningful participation and involvement. This is especially true for students, the predominant view being that they are "clients" rather than members or that they are too young to be serious participants in schoolwide, or even classroom-based, decision making. It is also a problem for educators, in part because of a stark differentiation in roles and status differences between teachers and administrators in most schools. In addition, the way the workday is defined leaves little room or motivation for cooperation or schoolwide participation. Furthermore, reward systems emphasize individual performance.

What can be done to shift the balance toward effective participation for both students and educators, as well as families and other members of the school community? To start with, the perception of students (and their families) as clients must be changed. Students as workers, families as important partners, and teachers as coaches must be promoted. This concept moves students and families from consumer roles at the perimeter of the action into the roles of primary actors in the educational process. This attitudinal change facilitates the full participation of everyone in the school community. For truly meaningful participation, students, families, and educators need to a) believe that they are doing things that matter; b) be challenged to contribute to their fullest capacity; c) recognize the value of participating and cooperating; d) have a sense of the impact of overall organizational dynamics on their own futures; e) feel free to probe assumptions; f) treat each other with respect; and g) be encouraged to experiment and take risks (Senge, Kleiner, Roberts, Ross, & Smith, 1994, p. 51).

The suggestions detailed above can help schools become resiliency-building organizations. Figure 4.2 summarizes the characteristics of such schools.

In Conclusion

Schools *can* achieve the profile shown in Figure 4.2. For many schools, however, this will require concentrated change efforts. The second half of this book turns to this topic: successfully engaging in the change process necessary for effective resiliency building to occur in schools.

Activities

1. Review the descriptions of Hay Elementary School and North High School. From these descriptions, identify how the six resiliency-building factors are demonstrated in these two school settings.

2. As an initial step toward resiliency building it is important to develop agreements about the current culture of the school. As a way of stimulating this dialogue, the use of metaphors can be powerful.

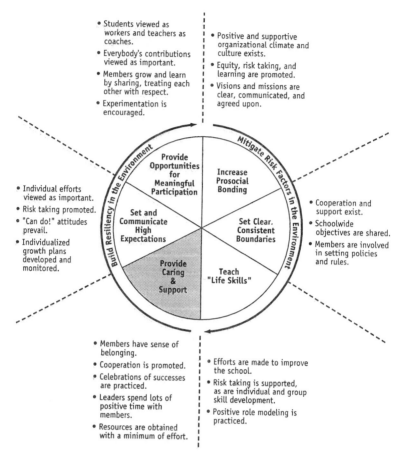

- Students viewed as workers and teachers as coaches.
- Everybody's contributions viewed as important.
- Members grow and learn by sharing, treating each other with respect.
- Experimentation is encouraged.

- Positive and supportive organizational climate and culture exists.
- Equity, risk taking, and learning are promoted.
- Visions and missions are clear, communicated, and agreed upon.

- Individual efforts viewed as important.
- Risk taking promoted.
- "Can do!" attitudes prevail.
- Individualized growth plans developed and monitored.

- Cooperation and support exist.
- Schoolwide objectives are shared.
- Members are involved in setting policies and rules.

- Members have sense of belonging.
- Cooperation is promoted.
- Celebrations of successes are practiced.
- Leaders spend lots of positive time with members.
- Resources are obtained with a minimum of effort.

- Efforts are made to improve the school.
- Risk taking is supported, as are individual and group skill development.
- Positive role modeling is practiced.

Figure 4.2. Profile of a Resiliency-Building School

Ask members to fill in the missing elements of the following phrase: My organization is like _____ because _____. Sharing the completed metaphors can be quite helpful in establishing the extent to which members view the school to be one that promotes resiliency. If the dominant metaphors are ones that depict a non-resiliency-promoting school, write examples of metaphors that might typify a resiliency-building school.

3. Identify the resiliency-building factors present in your school as well as the areas that need improving, based on Figures 4.1 and 4.2. Share your thoughts with your colleagues and encourage them to engage in a discussion about which of these factors are present in your school and which ones are absent or need improving.

5

Changing Schools
to Build Resiliency

There is a growing recognition that change is a process, a quest for improvement rather than a search for a final resting place.

JOSEPH MURPHY AND PHILIP HALLINGER
(1993, p. 255)

The second half of this book is devoted to helping schools develop effective responses to the critically important issue of resiliency building. This chapter outlines the basic framework and process for this effort, focusing on three activities that help establish an understanding of the status quo—assessment, agreement, and setting a course of action, and three activities that can change the situation positively—intervention, evaluation, and ongoing approaches. This framework, which follows the typical diagnostic-intervention-evaluation process of organization development (see Schmuck & Runkel, 1994), is more fully detailed in the following chapters. Later chapters also provide suggestions to help you apply this process in your school.

Understanding the Status Quo
and Deciding What to Change: Assessment,
Agreement, and Setting a Course of Action

People need to understand why the current state is not satisfactory before they will be willing to take the risks required to change and grow. They also need to know the specifics of their current situation so that they can set appropriate priorities and make reasoned choices in remaking their schools into more effective resiliency-building organizations. The more those involved—students, their families, educators, and other stakeholders—participate in the clarification of the current situation and the decision to take appropriate action, the more likely it is that ownership of the change process will occur. The processes described under the headings of assessment, agreement, and setting a course of action are intended to promote shared perceptions and widespread commitment to actions identified.

Assessment

The first step in the process is to assess the current state of affairs. The categorical areas that need to be assessed are the six resiliency-building factors that have been described in the first half of this book. Table 5.1 is a form that can be used to collect information about each of the factors on the Resiliency Wheel.

There are a variety of ways that this can be done.

1. Participants (combinations of students, educators, parents, and other stakeholders, depending upon purposes and needs) can gather together for a brief introduction to the concept of resiliency and the six factors included on the Resiliency Wheel. This can be followed at the same meeting with information gathering, which can be done by simply asking individuals to share their perceptions of the current state of affairs for each of the six factors in Table 5.1. Small groups can discuss their perceptions and record agreements, or a large-group discussion can be facilitated with agreements recorded for future use.

2. A committee can be formed to gather the necessary information. The committee can facilitate focus groups (Krueger, 1994) that explore participants' beliefs about the current state of affairs, or it can interview representative individuals. The committee can also use a survey, such as Figure 8.2, Assessing School Resiliency Building, included in chapter 8, to achieve the same purpose. The survey can be distributed to participants, collected, and results can be collated for later dissemination.

3. An outside resource person or group can be called upon to gather the information through one or both of the above activities.

TABLE 5.1 Resiliency-Building Factors for Students and Staff:
Assessing the Current Situation

1. Opportunities for bonding

2. Clear boundaries

3. Life skills

4. Caring and support

5. High expectations

6. Opportunities for participation

The advantages of this approach are the fresh perspectives, experience in facilitation, and skills that an outside person or group brings. The disadvantage is that it can reduce the potential for members "owning," or being committed to, the information collected. These trade-offs have to be taken into account when deciding how to proceed.

Regardless of which approach is taken, information gathering is the basic intent. Those involved in the effort will likely use some combination of the following methods (Milstein, 1993).

INTERVIEWS

Advantages: Easy to design; potential for much information; flexible use; potential for building trust.

Disadvantages: Difficult to quantify results; take much time to do; open to interviewer bias.

QUESTIONNAIRES

Advantages: Easy to quantify; much output for little effort; can be objective.

Disadvantages: Amount of time to prepare; not flexible; not able to pursue information in depth.

OBSERVATION

Advantages: Depth of information obtained.

Disadvantages: Open to bias in recording and analyzing information; amount of time required to do them.

RECORDS AND DOCUMENTS

Advantages: Easy to design and control the process; efficient use of time.

Disadvantages: Documents may not have necessary depth of information (public versus real data).

Agreement

The second step is to move toward agreement about the current state of affairs, validating and celebrating what is already being done well and deciding what is important to change. Activities include the following.

1. Helping participants to collate information collected in ways that provide clarity and understanding. This activity involves, as described above, gathering relevant information—for example, developing and administering questionnaires, conducting interviews, and analyzing documents. It then means effectively organizing the information obtained in ways that allow participants to "massage" it for understanding—for instance, developing charts and tables, summarizing feedback, and categorizing trends.

2. Presenting the collated information for review by all participants, as well as others who have a stake in hearing what has been gathered. They can then talk about the information and come to agreement about the current state of affairs—what is being done well and what, if anything, should be improved. This task, usually referred

to as survey feedback (see Bowers & Franklin, 1977; Nadler, 1979), includes three steps: a) organizing the information in ways that will enhance the likelihood of understanding—visual displays such as graphs and charts help ("a picture is worth a thousand words"); b) sharing and discussing it in an open meeting where members can clarify meaning and relevance; and c) encouraging the group to derive conclusions, celebrate what is already being done well, agree on priorities, and move toward a course of action. Whether all of this can or should be done in a single meeting depends on the time available and the extent of discussion that is required.

A step that is often overlooked in the process is taking adequate time to celebrate what is already happening that is effective. Resiliency building means recognizing strengths—what is being done well—and building on those strengths. School staff often are more motivated to make improvements when they are appreciated and recognized for what is already going well. Furthermore, an understanding of how district initiatives, such as cooperative learning, site-based management, full inclusion, and effective parent-community partnerships, build resiliency also can increase a commitment to these existing change efforts. Finally, such identification and celebration underscore the important point that effective resiliency building is not another add-on, but a foundation for effective education.

Setting a Course of Action

The final activity in the first half of the change effort is to figure out what directions need to be taken. If the first two activities are done effectively, clarification and agreement about the nature of existing strengths and shortcomings will have been established. What is required now is to develop an agreed-upon set of strategies to move from today's gap to tomorrow's improvement in the resiliency-building capacity of the school. At this point, an understanding of strategies that have the potential for overcoming specific resiliency-related barriers is required. Figures 5.1, 5.2, and 5.3, which focus on students, educators, and educational organizations, respectively, provide ways of thinking about this relationship between barriers and strategies. Specifically, these figures can be used to help participants make the necessary linkages between any barriers to resiliency that they agree exist and possible strategies that might positively affect these barriers. The figures are by no means comprehensive. Rather, they can be used

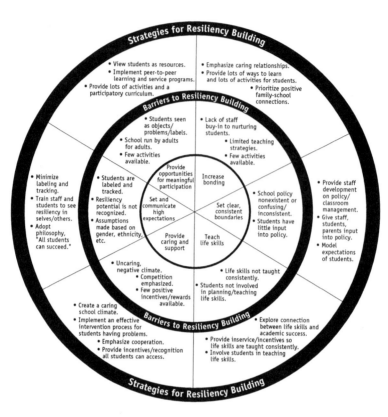

Figure 5.1. Fostering Student Resiliency: What Schools Can Do

as a starting point, a stimulus, for identifying further strategies that will help in particular school settings. You can drop, add, or otherwise modify items identified as barriers and strategies according to the realities of your situation.

It is important to include students in the process. Because of their unique vantage point, the most accurate picture of what is positive and what needs improving in building student resiliency often comes from this group. In addition, including students as active partners provides a resiliency-building activity in and of itself—an opportunity for meaningful participation in the school community. It also enhances the likelihood that they will be able to share the resources they have to offer the change process.

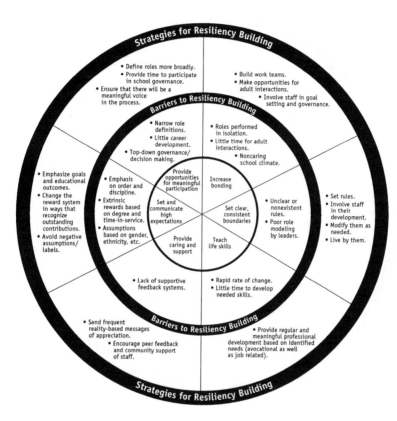

Figure 5.2. Fostering Educator Resiliency: What Schools Can Do

Changing the Situation Positively:
Intervention, Evaluation, and Ongoing Approaches

With a clear and agreed-upon picture of what the situation is and a sense of what can be done about it, the second half of the effort can be set in place: changing the situation to improve resiliency building. As with the first phase—clarification and decision to act—members of the school community need to be highly involved and take responsibility for the course of action that is undertaken. This is important because it increases the likelihood of risk taking and commitment to the changes that may occur.

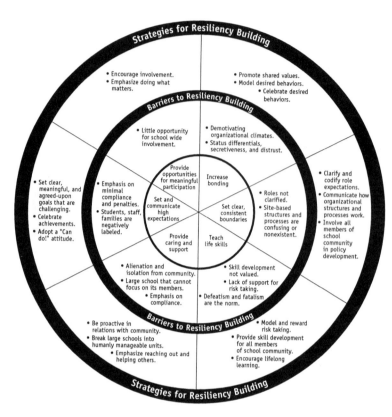

Figure 5.3. Resiliency-Building Schools: Making Organizational
            Changes

Intervention

Changing the situation in hopes of achieving greater resiliency is,
in and of itself, another resiliency-enhancing process. People learn,
change behaviors, and modify attitudes as a result of direct, shared
experiences. Thus, in a sense, the process is the product. The specific
objectives and strategies of the intervention will depend on the results
of the assessment and the agreements reached, as well as the target of
the needed changes—students, educators, or the school as a whole.
Three hypothetical examples are outlined below.

1. *Students*. The assessment may reveal a lack of consistently high expectations for student achievement and student success. In this case, it is important to reexamine policies and formal and informal practices related to tracking and labeling students, provide professional development that helps educators recognize the strengths of the different learning styles students bring to their education, and encourage the development of personalized instructional strategies that capitalize on them.

In the spirit of the Pygmalian effect—that is, people behave and perform in ways that others believe they will (Rosenthal & Jacobson, 1968)—it is important to promote changes in beliefs regarding students' potential for success. One way to intervene in this situation is to allow staff, students, and parents to visit other schools that are successfully dealing with this issue or to bring people from such sites to the school to share how they have successfully overcome similar barriers to resiliency building.

2. *Educators*. The assessment may reveal that many educators at the school feel depleted and ineffective and that their pedagogical skills are out of date. This may be due to some combination of changes in society, the expectations placed on schools, and the lack of meaningful professional development opportunities. If so, a decision to focus on improving life skills for educators can enhance their resiliency. The appropriate intervention will focus on identifying critical growth needs, both professional and personal, and delivering them in a way that encompasses adult learning principles (Levine, 1989).

3. *Schools*. The assessment may reveal that, universally, few opportunities exist for meaningful participation for students and most educators in the school. In this situation, it is important to take actions that focus on increasing involvement at all levels. For students, this may mean a major shift in instructional format in ways that promote proactive engagement ("student as worker"). For educators, as well as students, it may mean promoting questioning, critiquing, and two-way feedback, and establishing forums and times when this interaction can occur.

The assessment likely will result in the conclusion that there are some areas in which resiliency building already is in place and that there are some areas that need to be addressed. It is important that interventions be holistic—that is, responsive to *all* the realities that are identified and agreed upon, focusing on all aspects of student, educator, and school resiliency-related assessment outcomes. The problems that exist are interrelated and need to be dealt with in tandem. However, it is important to break the interventions into manageable steps, prioritizing and implementing them in a sequential manner. A consistent, step-by-step approach to making changes while celebrating successes along the way ultimately will be more successful than taking on too much, too fast, and becoming overwhelmed.

Evaluation

Will changes such as those identified above lead to the hoped-for improvements in school resiliency building? This is the goal, but there is no way of documenting its successful accomplishment, or of making changes along the way that may be required to "stay on target," unless efforts are monitored and evaluated. Evaluation needs to take place *during* the change process to ensure that things are going as planned (formative) and *after* the strategies have been put in place to ensure that outcomes are as intended (summative). As with the earlier steps in the process, the more partners included, the more likely that conclusions will be agreed upon and will form the foundation for support of further interventions that may be required. In addition, evaluation data are increasingly critical in obtaining the additional financial resources necessary to fund agreed-upon interventions.

Evaluation should be guided by a few important rules (Milstein, 1993).

1. *It should be purpose-driven.* Too often evaluations are viewed as superfluous—serving other peoples' needs or not having a focused intent. The exercise of agreeing on what is to be achieved establishes a meaningful basis for evaluation. This can be facilitated by tracking back to the results of the initial assessment, thus ensuring that the group stays on target. For example, if the initial concern is lack of expectations for high performance on the part of students, changing these expectations should be the driving purpose and form the basis of the evaluation effort. In other words, evaluation should test things that matter to the partners. It should focus on "what's important, what deserves focus, and what we expect as good performance" (Herman, Aschbacher, & Winters, 1992, p. 3).

2. *It should include evaluation of both governance and educational factors.* Governance factors are the structural and role modifications

that are intended to increase motivation and cooperation to build resiliency throughout the entire school. Educational factors are the instructional and curricular modifications that are aimed at resiliency building for students. Participants need to know the extent to which both kinds of modifications are happening.

3. *It should use the most appropriate assessment tools.* The idea is to discover whether processes or outcomes are occurring as anticipated. Standardized instruments are not likely to be focused or flexible enough to meet this need. Further, if sufficient training is provided and if appropriate assessment approaches and instruments (e.g., interviews, questionnaires, observations, review of documents, focus groups) can be developed, those who create them will be more likely to understand them and be supportive of the processes involved. The guiding principle is not elegance but effectiveness.

4. *It should not lead to undue fear and anxiety.* Evaluation does not have to lead to fear of reprisal when results indicate a need for further efforts, if those involved at all levels of the organization understand that they are engaged in significant change activities that likely will need to be modified over time as results are obtained. This is the nature of engagement in change processes. Nor does evaluation have to induce undue anxiety about learning how to conduct evaluation methods. It pays to follow the KISS principle ("keep it simple, stupid") and provide technical and secretarial help to ensure that members' time and priorities will not be unduly infringed upon.

Teachers and other school staff increasingly are recognizing their value as generators of useful knowledge for schools through an emerging research paradigm that involves the steps described above. Termed "practitioner research," this model calls upon school staff to become more systematic in what they already do—assess a current situation, decide on changes to improve the situation, evaluate the outcomes of the intervention, and start the spiral over again (Figure 5.4). Practitioner research is "insider research" done by practitioners using their own sites as the focus of study.

It is a reflective process, but is different from isolated, spontaneous reflection in that it is deliberately and systematically undertaken . . . [and] is oriented to some action or cycle of actions that practitioners wish to take to address a particular situation. (Anderson, Herr, & Nihlen, 1994, p. 2)

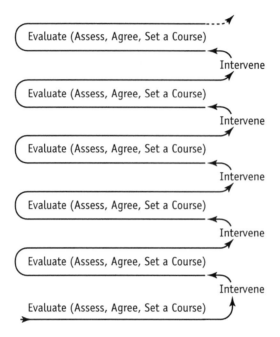

Figure 5.4. The Action Research Cycle for Practitioners
Source: Adapted from Anderson, Herr, and Nihlen, 1994

"Teacher as researcher" is enhancing or replacing traditional staff development models, challenging the notion that university-generated knowledge is the only useful form of research for educators, and providing another area of educator-student empowerment that is useful for resiliency building.

Ongoing Approaches and the Resiliency Model

It is one thing to agree on and pursue important resiliency-enhancing changes. It is quite another thing for them to become ongoing approaches, or *institutionalized*. For changes to become ongoing—a way of life—for students, educators, and the school, constant monitoring, modifying, and encouraging is required. This process is the responsibility of *all* those involved if it is to be embedded in the culture of the school. Further, it is important to understand that it will take time for this to occur, perhaps as much as 5 to 10 years before the changes become a way of life for the school and its members (Fullan, 1991). For many schools, this will require a major shift in mind-set from the typical "Band-aid, fix it fast" approach to one that is more realistic, long term, and comprehensive.

How does this come about? Mainly, it requires an understanding that resiliency building is an ongoing activity that requires continuing, constant, and focused attention over time. In fact, the six-step change process that has been described in this chapter is best viewed as a recycling set of activities as depicted in Figure 5.4. Status quo clarifications lead to positive changes that, in turn, require a new set of status quo clarifications and further efforts to promote positive changes, and so on. It is certain that students and staff will continue to encounter challenges and stresses over time. Therefore, the extent to which resiliency-building factors exist in the school must be continuously assessed and improved to facilitate student and staff resiliency in the face of these challenges. Without this ongoing cycle of assessment and improvement, maladaptive or dysfunctional coping patterns often replace the development of resiliency.

In Conclusion

Chapter 5 offers a basic approach to changing schools so that resiliency is developed in students, educators, and as an integral part of schools. The emphasis is on understanding and agreeing on the current situation and then moving on to make appropriate changes that contribute to the development of resiliency. The same structure can be used to assess and improve student, educator, and schoolwide resiliency building.

How can you apply the steps that have been introduced? Drawing upon examples of how schools—and an entire district—have actually implemented this process, chapter 6 focuses on ways that you can put the change process into action. Chapter 7 provides examples of specific resiliency-building "products" that have been developed within individual schools. Finally, chapter 8 provides a "tool kit" of ideas and activities that you can use in actually initiating and sustaining the process of resiliency building at your site.

Activities

1. Share information about the six resiliency-building factors on the Resiliency Wheel with others at your school. Distribute Table 5.1 and ask them to identify what is already being done in each of the six areas and what is important to work on regarding students, educators, and the school as a whole. This activity can help in determining if a basic agreement exists about the current status of resiliency building in your school and if a commitment to engage in further resiliency-building activities is present.

2. Administer the assessment questionnaire, Assessing School Resiliency Building (Figure 8.2), included at the end of chapter 8, to adults in the school (and, if appropriate, modify it for students and/or parents). Organize a "survey feedback" session as described in this chapter.

3. Survey members of your school community to determine the skills and knowledge that exists in your organization related to the six change process steps described in chapter 5. Based on the results of the survey, you may decide to establish a team to guide the process outlined in this chapter.

4. Discuss with your colleagues the concept of "educator as researcher." What are the limitations of the university as researcher-disseminator model? Has it worked in your school? What additional skills and resources do you need to access for educators in your school to engage in practitioner research?

6

The Change Process in Action

Early Opportunities became a basis for all the restructuring efforts at our school. From our gatherings where we . . . looked at resiliency issues, we had that as the basis of what we needed to do to improve the environment, the classrooms, the teaching at our school.

ALBUQUERQUE PRINCIPAL LINDA HUDSON IN THE
VIDEO *HOW SCHOOLS ARE CREATING RESILIENT
CHILDREN: THE ALBUQUERQUE PUBLIC SCHOOLS
EARLY OPPORTUNITIES PROJECT*
(HENDERSON & KINDERWATER, 1994)

Applying the process of change outlined in chapter 5 is the focus of chapter 6. Details about the change process are included, and several case examples of how schools have implemented resiliency-building change are examined. Relevant lessons are included from an Albuquerque, New Mexico districtwide 46-school, 3-year project directed by coauthor Henderson, which focused on integrating resiliency building into the fabric of schools. This chapter also provides questions you can use to put the process into action in your school.

The Albuquerque Public Schools
Early Opportunities Project

Albuquerque Public Schools (APS) received a $250,000 grant from the U.S. Department of Education (USDE) in 1991 to accomplish the historically elusive goal of integrating prevention and intervention efforts aimed at overall student wellness with efforts aimed at student academic success. Specifically, the project goal was to integrate the latest information on reducing youth risk behaviors and building student resiliency with ongoing school restructuring already taking place. Information about the project is included throughout this chapter for two reasons: to provide a model of a districtwide resiliency-focused change initiative and to share the lessons learned in the project so that other schools can benefit from both the project's successes and areas identified as needing improvement.

Though this project was funded to focus on student resiliency building (because recognition of the importance of and connection to educator resiliency is just emerging), the lessons described are relevant to resiliency-building for either students or educators.

Project Design

In the fall of 1991, the APS student assistance team sent out invitations to all elementary schools in the district (more than 80) to apply to participate in the project. The project plan was to work with about 40 schools over a 2-year period and add as many additional schools as funding permitted in the third year. In the fall of 1991, 20 schools responded with completed applications indicating interest in the project and a willingness to abide by the requirements for participation; 20 more applied in 1992, and 6 more were added in 1993. The requirements included a school administrator committed to participating in the initial 3-day training and planning session and in follow-up activities, and a school team composed of representatives of different grade levels, functions at the school, and the parent community, also committed to participating in an initial 3-day session and follow-up activities. Follow-up activities included formulating an action plan based on the assessment, carrying out the specific interventions included in the action plan, and evaluating the process of the project in the school. In addition, the teams were required to provide a minimum of 2 hours of training to the entire school staff after they participated in the initial session.

Project Implementation

The 3-day training and planning session focused for the first day and-a-half on sharing resiliency research and the key concepts of resiliency building (with time for team reflection and processing of this information) and for the second day and-a-half on assessing how well the school was doing in resiliency building and agreeing on a course of action for improvement. Hearing from other project schools' staff as to how they had used the resiliency information to initiate school change was included in this initial 3-day process in Years 2 and 3 of the project.

The assessment process was conducted with someone on the school team acting as recorder, while the entire team informally discussed the six elements of resiliency building listed on a form similar to Table 5.1. Teams focused on the questions, "What are we doing well in these areas?" "What could we do better?" and "How could we do it?" Teams were also given a questionnaire similar to the assessment form, Assessing School Resiliency Building (Figure 8.2), included in chapter 8, to assist them in this process. The teams reached some level of tentative agreement on a course of action to increase resiliency building in their schools, integrating if possible with restructuring efforts already in place. They also formulated a tentative action plan as to how to accomplish their goals. The assessment, agreement, and action planning were tentative at the 3-day training and planning session because most of the school teams recognized the need to get additional input from the staff back at school. School teams used time allotted in the 3-day session to plan a more in-depth, schoolwide process of assessment, agreement, and action planning that they would initiate after the resiliency information sharing they would provide. Once back at school, they became, in effect, the committee that oversaw the resiliency-focused change process described in chapter 5.

Project Evaluation

The project included a process evaluation, which was the only requirement of the funding agency. This evaluation, conducted at the end of the project, used focus groups from a cross-section of the project schools and a questionnaire that was sent to every project school, with instructions that the school staff who had been most involved in the project should fill it out. The evaluation focused on finding out the numbers of school staff who had become familiar with the goals of the project, how useful the school staff found the project, and the areas of resiliency building staff identified as a focus for the future.

The ways that individual project schools supplemented this evaluation to make it more useful for them, as well as other lessons from the project about implementing evaluation, are included later in this chapter.

Ongoing Approaches

In addition to the initial 3-day training and assessment, the project schools received ongoing consultation from Henderson and other district student assistance team staff and a newsletter about what schools were doing in the project and upcoming related training. Two booster trainings also were provided each year, based on input solicited from project schools as to their ongoing needs. In Years 2 and 3 of the project, schools that had excelled in implementing resiliency-building interventions were invited to present what they had done, both at the initial 3-day training and at the booster trainings. Money was provided for school teams to visit other schools to observe successful interventions in actual practice and for school teams to provide inservices to other school staffs on specific interventions.

Project Replication

Several school districts and individual schools in other parts of New Mexico and in other states have replicated the APS project, with modifications necessary for such a project to be most useful in each specific district and school. Many districts have used federal Safe and Drug-Free Schools or Title I monies, or both, to fund their efforts. Santa Fe Public Schools funded their resiliency project by submitting a grant proposal to a local private foundation.

Initiating Resiliency-Focused Change
in Your School: Determining Readiness

The design of the APS project ensured that some level of readiness was in place in the schools before they began a learning and change process related to resiliency. Several individuals in the school, including the school administrator, signed an application form agreeing to the ongoing process. Readiness for change is important to evaluate as you begin to initiate a similar process in your school or in your district. The following questions are useful to ask in evaluating readiness:

- "How open are the staff and administration in this school to starting a resiliency-focused change process?"
- "What can be done to increase that readiness?"
- "Are people feeling overwhelmed by other change initiatives or other challenges unique to this school?"
- "Whom can I get to be an informal (or formal) support group for me as I strategize what path to take in sharing the resiliency literature and initiating change to make our school more effective in resiliency building?"

In the APS project, people had a built-in support system in the team that went to the initial 3-day training and planning session. Project teams struggled with these questions as they mapped out plans to get buy-in for a long-term resiliency-focused change process back at their schools. One team from a school in which the principal had been suffering from a serious chronic disease (alternately coming to school and spending time in the hospital over several months) decided that the best thing they could do at the time was to nurture themselves as they grappled with this difficult challenge. Several other school teams decided that schoolwide initiatives already in place in their schools—such as cooperative learning, implementation of multiple intelligences-focused learning, increasing parental involvement in the school, implementing alternative assessment, and working toward more inclusion of special education students—were so connected to resiliency building that the best approach for their schools was simply to expand on these projects.

The survey-feedback procedure described in chapter 5 is one way to increase readiness. In this approach, you might decide to share some information about resiliency, then administer the assessment, Assessing School Resiliency-Building (Figure 8.2), included in chapter 8, or engage in a less formal process, such as the one described in chapter 5, using Table 5.1. Another strategy, employed by several of the project schools' teams, is simply to share brief pieces of the resiliency literature over many months, with an emphasis on what is already happening in the school that aids in resiliency building. At some point in this process, members of the group learning about resiliency may "spontaneously" identify areas of improvement to work on in the future.

An ineffective approach to developing readiness is to read a book or attend a conference or training and march into school with the attitude, "Boy, do we need to change some things around here!" People immediately resist this approach because of the implications that what they have been doing is wrong and that an entirely different change process is needed. A more effective strategy, mentioned above, is to tie resiliency building with other school initiatives that may be in process. In many of the project schools, an understanding of the resiliency literature increased buy-in to these initiatives by those in the school community who previously had been only "lukewarm." The resiliency focus shed new light on the need for these initiatives.

Initial Information Sharing

Before it is possible to assess how well your school is doing at resiliency building, groups in the school must understand the research and theory that form its foundation. In the APS project, this information sharing was accomplished in several ways. As indicated above, project schools selected a team of about eight individuals who represented various grade levels, other roles, and parents at the school, who attended the initial 3-day training and planning session. One of the requirements for schools to be a part of the project, which was explained in the invitation for application, was for school teams to return to school and share a minimum of 2 hours of information with the rest of the school staff. The follow-up evaluation of the project revealed that, in fact, almost 90% of the educators in each of the 46 schools participated in this minimum training.

Several school teams planned creative ways to present this information themselves to the rest of their school staff and parent and student groups; other teams elected to use Henderson as the project director or to bring additional outside trainers to their schools to present the information. Some of the schools most successful in implementing a long-term resiliency-focused change project offered small modules of training, some as brief as 15 minutes and others up to 45 minutes, every week or every month for most the school year. Using this approach increased readiness for change; it also made clear some connections to other school initiatives that had not been immediately obvious. These schools were also the most successful in getting most of the school personnel "on board," as compared with schools that only provided the minimum requirement of a 2-hour training.

Answers to the following questions are useful in planning an initial resiliency-information sharing.

- "What can I (or we) emphasize that will increase interest?"
- "What type of training might be best received?"
- "Should I (or we) try to bring in an outside speaker who can talk about this?"
- "Is there a place I (or we) can slip some resiliency-focused information into something that is already planned?"
- "Can I (or we) use creative approaches like role-playing, teaser questions, or door prizes to get people more involved?"

The Assessment

The more people and groups that are involved in the assessment process, the more accurate the picture is of what is going well in the school and what needs improving, and the more likely it is that large numbers of individuals and various groups will commit to an on-going change process. Think of the assessment approaches you could use (referring to suggestions in chapter 5) to get as accurate a picture as possible about the state of resiliency building in the school. Handing out a list of the six resiliency-building factors and asking students, parents, and school staff, "What is this school doing well?" and "What can we do better?" is one simple way of initiating assessment. High school students in Albuquerque, when given this opportunity to comment, have lamented the lack of extracurricular opportunities and have also been critical of the lack of fair and consistent boundaries. When challenged to approach the school administration with their own plans for improvement, the most typical reaction from the students has been that their input is not welcome, so why try?—indicating a critical need for more opportunities for meaningful participation for students in the change process.

Though initially frightening, getting student input is one way to get a truly accurate picture of the school and can lead to the utilization of vast untapped reservoirs of creative solutions and energy as students are invited to help change the situation. The same can be said for the involvement of parents.

One of the APS project schools identified a need to get art, music, and other extracurricular activities back into the school years before the project, when these programs were cut in APS. Through a true empowerment of its parent community, which included giving parents an equal voice on the school governance committee, the school tapped a reservoir of resources for meeting its goals. Parents moved from traditional support roles of fund-raisers and bake-sale providers to providing numerous in-school and after-school opportunities for students, including a variety of art activities, field trips, musical experiences, library programs, and computer labs. They reported that they felt they were true partners with teachers and students in this school community.

In addition to bringing parents on board as partners with tremendous untapped resources in resiliency building at school, it is also important to provide parents with information about the resiliency-building process so that they can be resiliency builders at home.

The Agreement

If a climate of open communication exists at a school, it is often the case that widespread agreement will be reached about what the school is doing well and what it could improve in resiliency building. If there is significant disagreement, the first step in the change process simply may be an ongoing discussion to better understand why people see the same situation so differently. Even if everyone cannot agree on everything, it is usually possible to reach agreement on some things that everyone will support in an ongoing change process. One way to facilitate agreement is to observe any issues that most staff (or, even better, staff, students, and parents) are concerned about.

The principal of one Albuquerque alternative high school noticed that the one issue most staff in her school were concerned about was student attendance. She saw this concern as an opening to begin a change process that had the potential to affect other areas of the school as well. Though addressing resiliency building holistically is the ideal, sometimes you must start wherever you can start, with the goal of moving beyond the initial focus on one problem.

In the elementary-focused APS Early Opportunities Project, the two areas that schools most often reported they were doing well were providing caring and support and opportunities for prosocial bonding. (In working with a number of secondary schools in addition to the APS project, we have found that these are often areas that are most in need of improvement at the secondary level.) The two areas project schools assessed as needing the most improvement were clear and consistent boundaries and teaching life skills. Though the project teams were representative of a broad cross-section of the schools, almost every team in the project agreed that they could not reach a final agreement on what changes to pursue until they involved their entire staffs in learning about resiliency, assessing the current status of the school, and discussing where the school needed to go.

In reaching agreement about what is being done well and what changes could be made in your school, it may be important to use someone within or outside the school with skills in facilitating this type of process. Various tools and activities can be used, some of which are included in chapter 8, to more effectively facilitate reaching agreement.

Setting a Course of Action

Once agreement is reached about what a school is doing well and what changes would make it more effective in resiliency building, setting a course of action simply means mapping out a path from where the school is now to where those involved in the process agree it should be. One way to do this is to use the "STP" process detailed in chapter 8: Write at the bottom of a piece of newsprint where the school stands now in the particular area of concern (the present situation); write at the top, stated as an accomplished outcome, where the group wants it to be (the target); and brainstorm about steps to get from the present situation to the target (the path). The steps can be prioritized after they are all recorded. Using a force field analysis, also included in chapter 8, which helps pinpoint what forces are working in favor of the proposed change and what forces are opposing it, also can be useful.

One important lesson learned in the APS project was the usefulness of getting "the power engine of the school" involved in both the assessment process and the process of charting and carrying out the actual interventions. That power may be the school governance council, the school improvement team, the school restructuring team, or a team that has another formal purpose but is, in reality, "the power engine of the school." Project schools that had this type of involvement were the ones that accomplished the most significant changes. Other schools where a peripheral committee tried to facilitate the change process were less successful. Many APS project schools actually sent their school governance teams to the initial training, which meant that from the beginning, the "power engine" of the school was on board, integrating the resiliency concept into other school endeavors.

Some schools were in the process of creating school vision and mission statements at the time of the initial training and planning session and decided that the key elements of resiliency should be included in those statements. Because long- and short-term goals were derived in APS schools based on the school vision and mission, integrating resiliency building into these statements proved to be one of the most successful approaches in maintaining a long-term resiliency focus. Two examples of these statements are included in chapter 7. Some schools decided to make resiliency building the major focus of their school. This meant that every significant decision and change in the school was evaluated in terms of its resiliency-enhancing potential. In these schools, the project goal of weaving student wellness into the fabric of the school was totally realized.

The Intervention Process

Brief case examples of three of the APS project schools are included in this section to illustrate the intervention process. Though most schools in the project implemented more than one intervention, single interventions are described in order to show more clearly this part of the change process.

Case Example Number 1:
Creating a Resiliency-Building School Policy

In this school, the team that attended the 3-day training and assessment process agreed that the school's student policy was inconsistent and, more important, provided nothing to assist students in changing their behavior if they got into trouble. This team included several members of the school governance team who reported this concern back to the entire school governance team, which also agreed this was a problem. This issue was discussed with the entire faculty, presented as a concern these two school teams had about students. The faculty agreed with the concern. The school counselor agreed to plan some intervention that might help this situation, with ideas and support from the Early Opportunities Project team. These interventions then were presented to the faculty as a whole for discussion, comment, and modification.

The counselor and her colleagues agreed that a resiliency-focused approach to school policy indicated the need to reward "good" behavior as much as intervening in "bad" behavior. They developed a policy that clearly spelled out a reward system for classes that had no member who violated any school rule for a semester. They clarified what those rules were and suggested a resiliency-building process to give students the skills they needed to abide by the rules in the future. Specifically, any student who broke a school rule was to be sent during lunchtime recess to the "Responsibility Room" where a peer mediator (the school already had an active conflict mediation program with trained student mediators) would assist the student in determining why he or she violated the school rule and what the student would do in the future when confronted with the same situation. Students who consistently wound up in the Responsibility Room were to be referred to the "Skillbuilders" program, where for six lunch recesses secondary students and the school counselor would train them in the skills they identified that would help them in the future. At the end of the 6-week session, the students would celebrate their learning at a pizza party, with pizzas donated by local businesses. Periodically, the counselor would touch base with the students after they "graduated" from Skillbuilders to see how they were doing with the skills they had learned.

The plan was presented, discussed, and modified slightly during several all-school staff meetings. In this case, the staff agreed on a needed change and gave authority to a small group of people—led by the school counselor who had the most professional expertise in the area of concern— to draft and present a plan of action, which was then implemented by the entire staff. A year later, the school counselor, principal, and teachers agreed that the new discipline policy, including the Responsibility Room and the Skillbuilders program had resulted in improved student behavior overall, and in fewer violations of school rules specifically. Evaluation of this program is discussed later in this chapter.

Case Example Number 2: Creating "Standards of Conduct"

A largely nonexistent school policy was also the arena of change in the second school. The team that went back to school after the initial 3-day training and assessment process decided to solicit information about this problem that they had identified from all the stakeholders in the school community. They facilitated classroom discussions with students about how they perceived the boundaries in the school and got useful and validating reports that rules were different room to room, teacher to teacher, and that the students were confused. They asked for and received similar reports from parents. They also asked for staff opinions about the issue. In the summer after the fall project training, they used money available from the project to provide stipends for a group of teachers who worked with parent volunteers to draft a code of conduct. The group decided that the code should be applicable to everyone in the school community, but worded in terms easily understood by students. A 14-item "Standards of Conduct" emerged from the summer meetings. After the faculty approved these standards, they facilitated discussions in their classes, allowing students to comment on and clarify each of the standards. The standards were then sent home with the students for the parents to sign and return to the school. A final creative step involved asking students to draw posters illustrating each of the 14 items, which were prominently displayed at student eye level near the entrance to the school. In this instance, too, after reaching agreement upon a course of action, the school community supported a smaller group who drafted the details of the intervention. However, everyone once again became involved when the intervention actually was implemented.

"Students are helping students now," said the school counselor of the new standards. "Before they would often say, 'I don't know' when asked about appropriate behavior. Now they do know, and they help each other abide by these standards of conduct" (from the video *How Schools Are Creating Resilient Children*, Henderson & Kinderwater, 1994).

Case Example Number 3:
Partnering to Provide Opportunities for Creativity

In the third project school, the team that attended the initial 3-day training and assessment process agreed that they wanted to continue an intervention they had begun 2 years prior to this project because of its close connection to resiliency building. Most students in this school come from economically disadvantaged families and the school staff had determined they wanted to expose the students to art, music, and other creative activities, even though funding for such programs had been cut by the district. The information shared in the Early Opportunities Project simply provided increased impetus for the school staff to partner with the University of New Mexico, using university music and art students to provide creative instruction and activities for students. In some instances, university students come to the school to provide regular instruction; at other times, the elementary students go to the university to use the musical instruments there in their instruction.

"You have to beg, borrow, and steal," the principal of this school said, only partially facetiously, in discussing this school's continuing efforts to find partners in the community to add opportunities for creative instruction and meaningful participation for students.

These case examples illustrate various approaches schools have taken to resiliency-building interventions. In deciding on specific interventions in your school, you will want to determine, as these schools did, who best could draft the details of the intervention once agreement is reached on a needed course of action.

Though many of the project schools did involve students and parents, most did not use them to their full potential. "What are all the ways students can be involved in designing and carrying out this intervention?" and "What are all the ways parents can be involved?" are important questions to ask in the intervention process.

Adult-Focused Interventions

As mentioned earlier, the Albuquerque Early Opportunities Project was a student-focused resiliency-building process. One of the lessons learned from the project is the importance of addressing educator resiliency in the process of building student resiliency. The project corroborated the point made in chapter 3: Overwhelmed, discouraged, or demoralized educators cannot be effective student resiliency builders. One of the goals of this book is to facilitate focusing on both students and educators as schools engage in increasing their resiliency-building capacity.

Evaluation

In addition to the overall project evaluation described at the beginning of this chapter, various evaluation techniques were used by project schools. In the school described in Case Example Number 1, the school counselor took on the evaluation process because of her interest in it. She explored comparing the total number of discipline referral slips generated in a school year before and after the implementation of the intervention; interviewing students who went through the Skillbuilders program as to its usefulness; and surveying faculty as to their observations about the effectiveness of the intervention. The school described in Case Example Number 2 also used faculty observation as an evaluation methodology. A more thorough and accurate evaluation would have included input from students and parents about the new code of conduct, gathered in interviews, focus groups, or surveys.

The example of the school presented in Case Example Number 3 presents a more difficult evaluation challenge. The staff of that school believed that exposure to a variety of in-school and extracurricular art and music activities would provide opportunities for students to connect (bond) with the school and with each other in prosocial ways, supporting resiliency building. They also believed that some students would develop competence at building self-worth in one of these areas, which would also further enhance resiliency. Questions this school staff has had to struggle with, as you will in your school, relate to each of the six resiliency factors in evaluation. They include the following:

- "How will we know when we have succeeded (in increasing bonds, teaching life skills, setting and consistently enforcing expectations, providing all students with caring and support, providing all students with high expectations for success, or providing all students with opportunities for meaningful participation)?"
- "What will success look like, feel like, sound like?"
- "What measures should we use?"
- "Who should we use them with?"
- "When should we use these measures?" (A useful form to use in this process, Worksheet for Evaluating Resiliency Building (Figure 8.4), is included in chapter 8).

It is important to hear the answers to these questions not only from school staff but also from students and parents, to create a more accurate evaluation process. Some schools, in fact, have sent students out with cameras and notebooks to document what effective learning looks, sounds, and feels like (Anderson, Herr, & Nihlen, 1994). This approach could also be used with any one or several of the six resiliency-building factors.

As is so often the case, the overall project process evaluation was conducted more to satisfy the funding source than to provide the most useful data for the school district. In retrospect, a more effective evaluation would have built-in ways to measure student and staff outcomes in terms of increased resiliency (interviews, questionnaires, use of secondary and artifactual data) and also would have included student and parent perspectives as to the effectiveness of the process in integrating resiliency building into the fabric of the school.

Ongoing Approaches

As mentioned above, the schools in the APS project in which resiliency building became integrated into the central purpose of the

school, as evidenced by buy-in from the "power engine" of the school
and inclusion in school vision and mission statements, are the ones
that sustained resiliency-building change process even when project
funding ran out. Almost all of the project schools, however, reported
that the ongoing support they received for the 3 years of the project
assisted them in maintaining a commitment to resiliency-focused
school change.

When funding for the project from the USDE ran out, it had been
discontinued altogether at the federal level. The district student assistance team staff brainstormed about additional ways to provide ongoing support for project schools. Henderson submitted a grant
proposal, which eventually was funded, to a different federal agency,
the U.S. Center for Substance Abuse Prevention (CSAP) for a different
type of project, a 600-person resiliency-focused conference. The conference was planned to feature all the major resiliency researchers in
the country, as well as APS and other schools that had developed
exemplary resiliency-focused strategies and programs. Through this
grant, which funded the conference "Moving Youth From Risk to Resiliency," held in January of 1995, some type of formal district support
for resiliency building was available for an additional year, and more
educators in the district bought into the concept of resiliency building.

Creativity is critical in maintaining the ongoing change process.
Because a successful change process can take 3 to 6 years or longer,
sustaining the momentum with the necessary money, training, and
other resources is a challenge. "How can we support the students,
staff, and parents involved in this process in the long run?" is an
important question to ask. "Can we use other community partners
like businesses or social service organizations to assist us in our
long-term efforts?" is another important, though often overlooked,
question. Many of the APS project schools invited their community
business partners to play a more active role in staff and student
resiliency building than just providing food or T-shirts, as they had
done in the past. Many business partners in APS were eager to play
an expanded role, which is probably the case in your community. A
daylong training on working together to improve resiliency building
was provided for project schools and their business partners during
the final months of the project, with the goal of schools' using those
business resources to maintain the resiliency focus when the project
funding ended.

In Conclusion

This chapter has described how an entire school district and several individual schools used the change process described in chapter 5 and has provided additional details about initiating a resiliency-focused change process. Questions that can be asked to guide the implementation process are included. The way each step in the overall process plays itself out needs to be tailored to the specific situation of your school, as it was in the APS project schools. Asking the questions included in this chapter, looking at the examples of specific products of the interventions schools have implemented included in chapter 7, and using the process tools in chapter 8 can assist you in facilitating a resiliency-focused change process most appropriate for your school at this time.

Activities

1. Find the natural allies in your school who you think will support resiliency building. Together, study the information about each of the steps in the change process discussed in chapter 5 and the examples in chapter 6. As a group, answer each of the change process-related questions included in this chapter.

2. Based on your discussion, chart a course of action, including each of the six steps of the change process, that you would be willing to facilitate. Discuss any reasons you hesitate to begin the process and how you might overcome your hesitancy.

3. Identify further reading, training, or other activities that might better prepare you to lead this process in your school. Discuss where you can get what you need.

7

Resiliency Building
in Practice

*Large changes occur in tiny increments. It is useful to
think in terms of a space flight: by altering the launch
trajectory very slightly, a great difference can be made over
time.*

JULIA CAMERON (1992, p. 144)

Several examples of specific approaches to increasing resiliency
building implemented by schools in the Albuquerque Early
Opportunities Project and other schools we have worked with—including artifacts these approaches have produced—are included in
this chapter. These examples represent only a few of the creative
approaches to resiliency building that schools have taken and are
included simply to stimulate thinking about possible creative interventions at your school. The best approach in any specific school is
one tailored to the educators, students, and community of that particular school.

The examples in this chapter primarily represent approaches to
student resiliency building because, as explained in chapter 6, educator resiliency building is just being recognized as an equally important and integrally connected focus. These examples are organized
with the most comprehensive approaches detailed first—school
vision and mission statements, schoolwide discipline policies, and
schoolwide incentive programs that reflect resiliency building. More
specific programs and approaches, including student assistance, conflict mediation, the inclusion of students in school governance, and
resiliency-building teaching strategies, are described next. Activities

suggested at the conclusion of the chapter can guide you as you develop specific resiliency-building approaches for your school.

School Vision and Mission Statements

As mentioned in chapter 6, several schools decided to include components of resiliency building in their school vision and mission statements, ensuring a weaving of the focus into the long-term future of the school. Two examples are shown below.

Mark Twain School

Mark Twain School Mission
Our challenge is to foster a love of learning, a positive and inclusive environment, [bonding, caring] acceptance of self and others, and a [boundaries] commitment to healthy lifestyle choices. [high expectations]

Our challenge is to foster a love of learning,
a positive and inclusive environment,   [bonding, caring]
acceptance of self and others, and a   [boundaries]
commitment to healthy lifestyle choices. [high expectations]

Our goal is to develop students who

- Are responsible decision makers   [life skills]
- Recognize and value individual
  differences and cultural diversity   [bonding, caring]
- Participate meaningfully in school and   [meaningful
  community, and   participation]
- Strive to reach their maximum   [high expectations]
  potential

A letter sent from the administrators of this school to parents and students at the beginning of the school year, with an invitation to serve on the school governance council, also embodies a resiliency-building message.

Welcome

Dear Parents and Students,

As we're sure you know, Mark Twain is a special place. The teachers are innovative and foster a love of learning through exciting and varied programs. The parents are committed to the importance of education and model their commitment through direct involvement with the school. The students of Mark Twain accept the strengths and weaknesses in one another and take pride in their own learning.

We are proud to be a part of this dynamic environment and pledge to maintain and advance the high standards of excellence at Mark Twain. As partners, we can keep learning alive and challenge each student to be the best they can be.

Please come by to visit and share your expectations, praise, and concerns.

Dr. Elizabeth Everitt, Principal
Dr. Catherine Snyder, Assistant Principal

Kit Carson School

The motto at Kit Carson Elementary school reads, "Where children are loved, because children come first!" The staff of this APS project school drafted a comprehensive list of beliefs [included here in an edited format] that became that school's resiliency-focused vision and mission statement.

We at Kit Carson Elementary School believe:

- All children can learn.
- Children are worthy of respect.
- Children learn by doing.
- Children learn in a safe, positive, supportive environment.
- Children are individuals who learn at different rates and ways.
- Children need to be encouraged and challenged.
- Children's self-esteem is built by recognizing their strengths which lead to better learning.
- Children learn best when they feel good about themselves and their parents are committed to their education.
- Children learn best in a stimulating and cheerful atmosphere where a lot of cooperation and respect are present.
- Children learn best if given an opportunity to experiment and discover solutions on their own.
- Children should be responsible for their own learning.

- Children learn best when their culture is respected and integrated into their learning.
- Children need to develop their own best intelligence because they each have special and unique qualities.
- Curriculum must be modified to students' learning abilities, culture, and past experiences.
- Children learn best when there is a connection between home and school, and when parents are actively involved in their child's learning process.

Resiliency-Building Approaches to Discipline

Kit Carson School

The staff of Kit Carson also developed the following guidelines for "preventive discipline" after their participation in the APS project.

Preventive Discipline
We believe that when students are actively involved and there is frequent communication, many discipline problems can be avoided. Some of the procedures and techniques used at Kit Carson in preventive discipline are:

1. Do not consider discipline as separate or apart from the rest of the teaching process.
2. Show genuine interest in all of your students and accentuate the positive.
3. Have well-defined rules (posted) as to what is expected of the children.
4. Be consistent in all things (presentation of materials, enforcement of the rules, etc.) so that the children know what is expected of them.
5. Emphasize respect for others—teachers, pupils, adults, property, and so on.
6. Share the good things the children are doing with others (the parents, administration, other teachers, and other children all like to hear and share in the successes of our students).

7. Cooperative schoolwide [preventive] discipline program:

    a. Gold Slips are given to students who behave properly. One Gold Slip—trade for popcorn. Ten Gold Slips in 9 weeks—lunch with the principal.

    b. Students who do not receive infraction notices each 9-week period will receive a prize.

    c. Conflict mediation is used.

    d. The school participates in TASA [student assistance] programs.

The school also formulated an extensive "corrective discipline" policy, which clearly outlined eight key school rules and steps taken for each number of infractions. Its primary focus on "preventive discipline," however, is a resiliency-building approach—accentuate the positive to alleviate much of the need for corrective discipline.

Another creative approach to discipline, designed to foster staff resiliency at Kit Carson, was the assignment of "buddy teachers"—individuals who could be called upon by other staff in the school in any "corrective discipline" situation. Through this approach, the staff built in caring and support for one another in what are often tense and stressful situations and ensured a greater likelihood of students being treated with caring and respect (through the intervention of a more neutral third party).

East San Jose School

East San Jose School developed a discipline policy based on the idea that every student had certain rights, and formulated it as a list of rights for students.

East San Jose Bill of Rights
1. Everyone has a right to be safe and no one will be hurt.   __ There will be no fighting, kicking, hitting, pinching, or pushing.   __ There will be no weapons at school.

___ Students will be at their assigned place at proper times.

___ Students will use all equipment properly and safely.

Consequences:

1st Offense: Time-out with mediation and contract [see below]. Days in time out determined by completion of contract.

2nd Offense: Time-out with mediation; parent contacted by classroom teacher.

3rd Offense: Time-out with mediation; conference with parent and principal.

2. Everyone has the right to be respected.

___ To dress appropriately.

___ Foul language will not be tolerated.

___ Destroying property will not be allowed.

___ Defiance is unacceptable behavior.

Consequences:

1st Offense: Time-out with mediation and contract. Days in time out determined by completion of contract. Restitution for vandalism or graffiti.

2nd and 3rd Offense: Same as above with possible School Police involvement.

3. Everyone has the right to be drug-free.

___ Alcohol, drugs, and tobacco will neither be used nor tolerated.

Consequences:

1st Offense: School Police and parents will be called, counselor referral, in-house suspension.

2nd Offense: School suspension.

4. Everyone has the right to be happy and treated with compassion.

___ We will not hurt each other's feelings.

Consequences:

1st Offense: Time-out with mediation. Days in time-out determined by completion of contract.

2nd and 3rd Offense: Same as above.

Students violating this policy are sent to this school's "Responsibility Room," where they meet with a student mediator (a peer with training in conflict mediation) and fill out the following contract.

My Contract and Plan

1. Why are you here in time out?

   _____

2. What is wrong with that behavior?

   _____

3. What will you do to keep this from happening again?

   _____

   _____ Student
   _____ Mediator
   _____ Parent
   _____ Date

Besides using the resiliency-building approach of formulating a student discipline policy based on a positive statement of students rights, including the rights of safety, respect, healthy lifestyle choices, and compassion, East San Jose's approach allows students violating the policy to take responsibility for figuring out how to stay out of trouble in the future, with the support and encouragement of a student role model.

Incentive Programs for All Students

East San Jose School

Two other approaches to resiliency building have been implemented by East San Jose. Convinced that every student's resiliency could be enhanced by providing opportunities for every student to be recognized in some way, the school initiated the "On a Roll" program as an alternative to the traditional "Honor Roll" program. In this program, school staff nominate students who improve over the term in academic work, behavior, or attendance. These students are then recognized at an all-school assembly, with their parents attending, as "on a roll to success." They receive a prize and their names are posted in the school cafeteria.

East San Jose's "Walk Tall" program is another way the school recognizes as many students as possible. Teachers in the school hand out the forms shown below as they notice students taking increased responsibility, showing respect to one another, and behaving politely. When students get five certificates, they get to sign a "Walk Tall" book kept at the school and participate in a celebration, such as an ice cream social.

Responsibility	
East San Jose Award	
__ CLASSWORK	__ BEHAVIOR
__ HOMEWORK	__ PROPERTY AND EQUIPMENT

Respect	
East San Jose Award	
__ KINDNESS	__ HELPFULNESS
__ TEAMWORK	__ COURTESY

Politeness	
East San Jose Award	
__ ASSEMBLY	__ CAFETERIA
__ CLASSROOM	__ PLAYGROUND

Cleveland Middle School

Several secondary schools have extended the "On a Roll" concept to involve businesses and organizations in the community. A vice-principal at Cleveland Middle School in Albuquerque asked students what they would most like for prizes in this type of school program— a program where every student has the opportunity to be recognized

and rewarded. Students generated a list of attractive awards like free
movie tickets, free meals in fancy restaurants, a limousine ride, and
discounts at local businesses. The administrator and staff then
scoured the community to find the awards. All students at Cleveland
who bring their grades up one grade point or improve attendance in
a semester are publicly recognized for their work, and their names are
placed in a drawing for the coveted prizes. Limousines pulling up to
the school to take students to local restaurants for lunchtime meals,
as the student body looks on, demonstrate the creativity of the staff of
Cleveland in providing incentives that students want and that every
student in the school has the potential to receive. One counselor at the
school commented, "I was amazed at how many of our 'trouble-
makers' signed up to participate in this program"—another testimo-
nial to the desire within almost everyone to increase his or her
success.

A Caring Approach to
Health-Compromising Discipline Violations

How does a school intervention ("Care" or "Core") team handle
students who are referred for serious or repeated violations of the
school's discipline policy? Two critical approaches to supporting
student resiliency building in these situations have been implemented by several schools. First, the intervention team focuses on the
strengths of students as well as their problems. Referral forms that
include equal space for identifying problems *and* strengths help ensure that the students' strengths are looked at in equal proportion to
the risks or problems. The team then poses this question in discussions about the student: "How can we use this person's strengths to
facilitate solutions to the problems?"

The second approach involves making sure that a student receives some help for his or her problem. Too often, schools send
students out the door, assuming they will somehow "be better" when
they return to schools days or weeks later. In reality, without increasing the web of protection diagrammed by the Resiliency Wheel, in all
likelihood the students' problems will get worse, and the overall
health of the school community, as well as that of the student, will
suffer. A resiliency-building approach adopted by many schools is to
require an assessment for alcohol, other drugs, or other significant
problems, administered by an in-school or outside agency trained

professional, as a stipulation for returning to school. Without this approach, the resiliency of the student and of the entire school community may decline.

Pojoaque Valley School District

The following statement of philosophy attached to the substance abuse prevention and intervention policy of Pojoaque Valley Schools in Pojoaque, New Mexico demonstrates a resiliency-building approach to student assistance.

> The Pojoaque Valley School District recognizes that alcohol and other drug use/abuse is a treatable health problem. Health problems of youth are primarily the responsibility of the home and community; however, the schools share that responsibility because use, misuse, abuse, and dependency problems often interfere with school behavior, student learning, and the maximum development of each student. The schools shall intervene with students manifesting a sign of use, misuse or abuse, and make a concerted and consistent effort to educate and assist them in obtaining appropriate services.

The consequences of violating the substance abuse policy are stated as a 2-day suspension and

> the student cannot be reinstated until a meeting is held with the principal, parent/guardian, student and others as deemed necessary by the Care Team. A no-use drug contract will be signed by the student and witnessed by the parent/guardian. As a part of the reinstatement, the parent must abide by the Care Team recommendation. This may include community service, professional drug use/abuse evaluation, counseling, etc. The parent/guardian and student will present a plan of action that is acceptable.

Conflict Mediation

Many elementary schools have conflict resolution programs in which all students and staff are trained in a conflict resolution curriculum and certain students act as conflict mediators, usually available during recesses and before and after school to mediate the conflicts of their peers. In 1993, however, one Albuquerque high school initiated a secondary-level mediation program that provides specially trained students with academic credit for their mediation activities.

Highland High School

Students in the mediation class at Highland High School, the first of its kind in the district, are available every period of the school day to mediate conflicts between their peers at school. About 150 conflicts were mediated by the students in 1993, and 95% of the agreements reached in the meditations were kept. Violence in the school decreased and administrators were involved in less disciplinary action. Mediator Bernarda Hernandez wrote of her experience:

> Mediation has caused me to think about the problems instead of just reacting and punching someone. I think of what's going to happen if I do something crazy when someone gets me mad . . . I think of the consequences it would bring.

Because the mediation process involves the disputants listening to one another, hearing one another's points of view, and coming up with a mutually agreed-upon solution in a five-step process (shown in Fig. 7.1) facilitated by mediators, it is resiliency building for all involved. APS Early Opportunities Project schools found an unexpected benefit occurred when their student mediators took the process home. Students began mediating neighborhood and family conflicts, based on their experience at school, causing numerous parents to contact the schools requesting mediation training for themselves.

Students on School Governance Teams

Several schools in the APS project placed students on their school governance councils, a move considered radical at the elementary level. The students, however, surprised school staff with their eagerness to serve, their creative ideas, and their high energy for change. Educators reported how amazed they were to hear the students' perspectives on the school and what good ideas they had. One school

The Process of Conflict Mediation
1. Mediators explain the roles and rules of mediation
2. Stage 1: Define the problem—parties describe their view of the situation (tell their story) and express feelings.
3. Stage 2: Mediators help parties to understand one another's points of view.
4. Stage 3: Find a solution—mediators help parties brainstorm and decide on a solution agreeable to both parties.
5. Closing: Mediators write down the points of the agreed-upon solution and have all parties sign.

Figure 7.1. The Five-Step Conflict Mediation Process
Source: Adapted from the New Mexico Center for Dispute Resolution, 620 Roma Ave. N.W., Albuquerque, NM 87102.

with a school governance team called the School Improvement Team formed a Student School Improvement Team, which at times met separately from the adult team, and at times met jointly with it. Those involved with the students had similar reactions to their participation—great ideas, wonderful creativity, high energy. Because only a minority of the staff supported this intervention, however, it was short-lived due to lack of widespread support. As is too often the case, students in this one project school wound up only tasting this level of participation at their school. Fortunately, other project schools maintained ongoing inclusion of students in school governance.

Teaching Strategies for Resiliency Building

One way to meet the challenge of resiliency building, implemented by several project schools, is to use teaching strategies that incorporate the six resiliency-building factors diagrammed in the Resiliency Wheel. Each of these factors is inherent in cooperative learning approaches that incorporate both an academic goal and a social skills goal in each learning activity. Although successful implementation of cooperative learning requires effective staff training and ongoing staff skill development, the rewards in terms of improved student wellness and student academic achievement are well documented (Fullan, 1991; Hawkins et al., 1992; Johnson & Johnson, 1989).

The service-learning approach to education includes within its structure the paradigm shift of resiliency building: Students are seen as resources rather than as utilizers of resources, actively engaged in learning rather than passively receiving someone else's knowledge, producing rather than consuming, offering help rather than always receiving help, and serving as leaders rather than followers or victims. Inherent in the process is not only academic accomplishment but the development of citizenship and other social skills, as well as an increased empathy for others, self-confidence, and a sense of belonging to the community. Effective utilization of this approach to education requires extensive training and ongoing problem solving, but schools implementing service learning report that the rewards in terms of student development (i.e., resiliency building) are worth the effort.

Other Examples of Student-Focused Resiliency-Building Interventions

Other student-focused interventions that have provided key elements of resiliency building, implemented in Albuquerque and elsewhere, include before- and after-school programs (especially for "latchkey" students), student support groups (ideally available to all who want or need them and structured in a nonstigmatizing way), cross-age tutoring and mentoring ("buddy" programs), student peer helper programs, leadership training programs that integrate both traditional and "nontraditional" student leaders, and many art, music, drama, sports, and other activities available to students during and after school.

In Conclusion

This chapter includes specific examples of programs and other strategies schools have used in increasing their effectiveness in resiliency building. The most comprehensive and institutionalized examples are the school vision and mission statements that included components of resiliency. Approaches to school discipline that focus on reinforcing positive student behaviors as well as clearly delineating unacceptable behaviors and their consequences also integrate several resiliency-building factors.

Your school, no doubt, already has in place some of its own programs and strategies that foster resiliency. Identifying what you are already doing that is building resiliency and expanding it or increasing its effectiveness is one place to start in improving your school's resiliency-building capacity. Chapter 8 provides specific "tools"—forms, activities, and processes—that you can also use in your school in the process of increasing individual and organization-wide resiliency building.

Activities

1. Identify programs and teaching strategies considered effective or innovative in your school. What components of resiliency building do they incorporate?

2. Consider how these approaches could be more effective resiliency builders. Think of ways you can facilitate these improvements.

3. Select examples of specific resiliency-building approaches included in this chapter that you would like to implement at your school. Using the information on initiating change included in chapters 5 and 6, map out a plan you can initiate to make these approaches happen at your school.

8

Tools to Facilitate Change

Tell me, I forget
Show me, I remember
Involve me, I understand

CHINESE PROVERB

The final chapter offers a variety of "tools" that can be employed to build resiliency and maximize involvement in necessary change efforts and increase the probability of positive results. The intent is to provide ideas that can be applied to your organization's change process. These ideas may need to be modified and others may need to be developed that are more appropriate to meet particular needs. This is to be expected. Long-term resiliency development requires inventiveness and adaptability.

The suggestions are organized into three categories—assessing the current state, promoting change and building commitment, and evaluating efforts and celebrating outcomes. As will be noted, some of the ideas are specifically intended for individual (student or educator) application or for organizational resiliency building, whereas others may be helpful for either purpose.

Tools for Assessing the Current State

These activities can help get the discussion started, identify points of strength and areas of need, and motivate participants to come to agreement about actions that need to be taken.

The Resiliency Wheel

The Resiliency Wheel can be used to create a common language, assess the status quo, and identify other things that need to be done. Distribute copies of the Resiliency Wheel to participants, review the six factors of resiliency building included on the wheel, and facilitate a discussion to be sure that everyone understands the meaning of each of the factors. This step helps to establish a common language that any group can use. Subsequently, the Resiliency Wheel can be used to take stock of the current state of affairs. For example, the group can discuss each factor, then come to agreement about what is presently happening that promotes or detracts from resiliency. Finally, the group can discuss what else needs to be considered to increase resiliency building.

As explained in chapter 1, the Resiliency Wheel also can be used for other assessment purposes. For example, teachers can view it as a Resiliency Web and use it with parents and students early in the school year to come to an agreement about the student's current state of resiliency and areas of the web that may need "more strands woven in." The agreements can be formalized as a contract among parents, teacher, and student. If portfolios are used as part of the instructional design, students can be required to include the resiliency-building goals that have been agreed upon as a part of that effort.

The Resiliency Figures

The resiliency figures introduced in chapter 5 also can serve to assess the status quo and identify future directions for resiliency building. The figures provide information about barriers and strategies that can be used to stimulate discussion. After the group gains familiarity and comfort with the Resiliency Wheel, they can use the figures effectively to assess the state of affairs at the site and, if warranted, identify what needs to be done to change things. The target can be students (Figure 5.1), educators (Figure 5.2), the overall school (Figure 5.3), or all three. Using the figures to start the conversation, the key questions to ask include "What are the barriers that keep us from building resiliency?" and "What strategies need to be considered to increase our ability to build resiliency?"

Assessing School Resiliency Building

This questionnaire was developed by coauthor Henderson as an informal instrument to assess perceptions about the current state of school resiliency building. It includes questions focused on students, educators, and the school and includes all six of the Resiliency Wheel's factors. It can be distributed at a meeting, scored by participants, and results can be collated quickly to develop an overall sense of beliefs about site-based resiliency. The group can analyze the results, draw inferences, and make decisions about next steps that may be required. The instrument, a copy of which can be found in Figure 8.2 at the end of the chapter, can be copied and used at the reader's site.

Assessing Educator Plateauing

This is a questionnaire that has been developed by coauthor Milstein to help educators assess their plateauing levels. Plateauing occurs most frequently when one a) becomes an "expert" and concludes that work life has become routine (content plateauing); b) senses that there is little opportunity for growth, status expansion, or promotion in the organization (structure plateauing); or c) feels that life is too predictable and not fulfilling (life plateauing). When one or more of these beliefs takes hold, it is difficult to be highly resilient. Therefore, it is important to understand the concept and assess participants' level of plateauing as a basis for developing motivation to take necessary resiliency-building actions. The plateauing instrument at the end of this chapter, Figure 8.3, can be used for this purpose. Respondents can score their own results on the form provided. If appropriate, results can be collated to develop a group picture that then can be used as a basis for discussion and decision making about resiliency building. The instrument can be copied and used at the reader's site.

Changing the Focus From Risks to Resiliency

This exercise helps to establish that everyone has inherent characteristics of resiliency, even those who are viewed as most "at risk." Ask participants to think of an individual they are worried about—a student, a fellow educator, or themselves (depending upon which of these groups is the focus of the exercise). Then have participants write the first name of this person on the top of a blank sheet of paper and draw a line below the name, dividing the page into two equal columns. Direct participants to record in the left-hand column three or four of the main reasons they are concerned about this person, considering internal factors such as attitudes and behaviors and external factors such as worrisome environmental conditions. Then, with instructions to be as thorough in the next step of the activity as they typically are in finding an individual's problems and risks, ask participants to identify and record in the right-hand column as many strengths or positives as they can in the life of this individual—both internal factors such as talents, potentials, attitudes, and behaviors and external factors such as people and other positive environmental influences. As a final step, share the seven resiliencies (Wolin & Wolin, 1993) and the other characteristics of resiliency detailed in Table 1.1, and ask participants to pair off and discuss whether any of the positives they identified connect with these characteristics of resiliency. Remind the group that resiliency increases by identifying strengths and focusing on them as much as or more than problems or risks, mirroring them to individuals, and using them as a focus for any needed interventions. As previously noted, the Pygmalian effect is powerful—how you see those you serve will have much to do with how they behave and respond (Rosenthal & Jacobson, 1968).

Y Charting

This is an exercise that is intended to encourage participants to move beyond intellectualizing and get in touch with their deeper feelings and concerns about resiliency building. It can be used to stimulate a group discussion about student, educator, or school resiliency building. Draw a Y on a piece of paper. Write "feel like," "look like," and "sound like" on the three edges of the Y. Give participants copies and ask them to add descriptive words in each area of the Y about either the current state or the hoped-for state of resiliency for students, educators, or the school. Have them share their thoughts in small groups, identify their agreements, and then share them in a large group setting.

Tools for Promoting Change and Building Commitment

These activities can be used to motivate the group to take necessary actions to change the status quo and increase resiliency building.

What's Excellent, OK, Not Being Done

This is a bridging activity between assessing the current state of affairs and moving toward commitment to change. It promotes a feeling of security—that effective programs and behaviors will be held safe while other things are being changed. Ask participants to list the things about their schools that they believe are excellent in promoting resiliency—things that should not be changed. After a discussion leads to agreements, ask them to focus on what is okay about the school regarding resiliency building but can be better if changes are made. Finally, ask the group to think about other things that promote resiliency that are currently not being done. The questions need to be put to the group in the order suggested to promote an atmosphere of security, which is necessary if the group is going to be candid and take necessary risks. The goal of this activity is agreement about particular actions that need to be taken to increase resiliency building.

Taking the Roof Off the Resilient School

Ask the group to imagine that they have gone through the efforts required to increase resiliency building in the school. It is now 10 years later. The group is to imagine they have removed the roof of the school and they are peering down into it to see what is going on. What do they see that indicates that the school is now more resiliency building? Ask participants to volunteer things they see (e.g., more student-initiated interactions, teachers modeling risk taking, hall exhibits that demonstrate high expectations). As a modification, the group could be asked to focus on each of the factors on the Resiliency Wheel as they peer down into the school.

Norming

Agreement about resiliency-building norms can help establish behaviors that model the group's goals. One way of establishing these norms is to distribute the Resiliency Wheel's six factors to the group. Then divide the members into six groups, one for each of the factors. Ask each group to identify norms that they think must exist to guide behaviors regarding the factor they have been assigned (e.g., to provide care and support, the group might recommend such norms as respecting and honoring each other's unique teaching-learning styles, making efforts to celebrate each other's birthdays, and sending condolences when there is a crisis). These norms can be shared, added to and modified as needed, and adopted by the group. If they are put into writing, they can be reviewed regularly, updated as needed, and shared with others who become members of the group at a later time.

Yours-Mine-Ours

This activity can help to clarify resiliency-building areas that the entire group of participants should take responsibility for putting into action and that should be the responsibility of particular role groups. It can help to clarify parameters. For example, what are the total group's responsibilities and prerogatives? What is best left to particular role players? Getting answers to these questions helps to delimit the agenda and keep the group on track while reminding those in particular roles—parents, students, teachers, and administrators— that activities that legitimately belong to them are their responsibilities and will remain under their control.

Each participant should be given sets of note cards—one for the total group and one for each of the role groups that are involved. Ask them to give a card a title with each particular role group's name (for example, "School Improvement Team") and list the resiliency-building activities that should be the responsibility of each group. Have them do the same for the entire group. Then have participants sort the cards into stacks for each role group and one stack for the whole group. Small groups can be assigned to review different card stacks and draw general conclusions. These can then be shared in the large group. Agreements can be recorded and disseminated.

Situation, Target, Path (STP)

This is exercise was developed by Schmuck and Runkel (1994). It can help a group to clarify the nature of resiliency-building problems, the goals to be achieved, and the strategies to achieve desired goals. The exercise helps participants to specify whether they need to focus on beliefs about the present situation (S), the goal or target (T), or the actions or path (P) to be used to get from the current situation to the goal. STP sessions, using the brainstorming approach described next for each of the three steps, allow the group to share perceptions and prioritize where and how to make changes.

Brainstorming

Resiliency building requires creativity because established behaviors and habits are hard to break. Brainstorming encourages participants to think without the shackles of the past holding them down. In the first stage, ask participants to suggest responses to a resiliency-building question or issue. (If using this activity in an STP session, participants would determine the current situation, then the target, and then the path.) Share guidelines for brainstorming with participants before you begin the activity—"let ideas just come," regardless of how impractical the ideas may appear to be; record all ideas, without criticizing or modifying; and, most important, tolerate silences, which are times when people "go inside" to think. In the second stage, ask the group to review the ideas that have been recorded. This is the time to become more analytical, drop ideas, modify others, and combine those that seem to go together. In the third stage, ideas that survive the review can be explored and decisions can be made to put them into action. This entire process can be used for each step in the STP process described above.

Consensus Decision Making

Resiliency is promoted by involvement in decision making. Participants need to learn to cooperate in clarifying issues and coming to decisions about what needs to be done. Consensus decision making is a powerful means of increasing commitment to actions that should be taken. It can also be a creative process that leads to better decisions, especially when members of the group have different experiences and understandings. Because it takes more time than majority or minority decision-making approaches, and more goodwill and facilitation skills, it should be reserved for those decisions that clearly require group understanding and commitment.

Consensus does not mean that everyone agrees about the decision. It does mean that everyone a) understands the issues; b) has been given opportunities to talk about how they feel about the issues and the possible solutions; and c) is willing to abide by decisions that are made, even if those decisions are not their preferred choices. If the group understands these basic rules and is given help in practicing consensus decision making, the quality of the decisions that are made will improve and norms of cooperation and trust will grow.

Force Field Analysis

This activity is detailed by Schmuck and Runkel (1994, pp. 258-259). It requires the group to identify the existing forces that facilitate or hinder the achievement of a goal (or target, in the STP activity). After listing these forces for each identified goal, the group should develop strategies to alter the balance of these forces—expanding the influence of those that help and mitigating the influence of those that hinder. This exercise encourages participants to further analyze important steps in accomplishing goals, break goals into smaller pieces that are more easily accomplished, focus on the goals that are most attainable, and better understand why attaining other goals may be difficult. Figure 8.1 can be used to assist in this activity.

Tools for Evaluating the Effort and Celebrating Success

These activities can help participants know whether they are making progress toward resiliency-building goals. The intent is to monitor the effort to keep it on track (formative), establish results (summative), and motivate continuing efforts.

Evaluation Worksheet

This worksheet, included in Figure 8.4 at the end of the chapter, draws participants' attention to the six resiliency-building factors and the information that needs to be collected to determine the extent to which they are being realized. The worksheet can best be used formatively, as a means of establishing an evaluation strategy—that is, estimating where things are presently and identifying indicators that can be used to establish results, measures that are required to get the

Target: Where we want to be _____

Helping Forces	*Hindering Forces*

Where we
are now

Ways to maximize
helping forces:

Ways to mitigate
hindering forces:

Figure 8.1. Force Field Analysis

necessary information, and an action plan for the effort. The worksheet can be copied and used at the reader's school site. With some modifications, the matrix also can be used to guide summative evaluation (e.g., instead of the column titled "What would it look like . . . ," it could read, "What does it look like . . . ").

Resiliency-Building Factors

To get some quick thoughts about current and needed resiliency-building outcomes, ask participants to fill out their impressions on a form that simply lists the six resiliency-building factors, such as Table 5.1. After everyone lists impressions, positive and negative, facilitate a discussion intended to reach agreement about the current state of resiliency building and what needs to be done to improve it.

Recognition

Recognition for efforts made and outcomes achieved facilitates further resiliency-building efforts. Recognition can take a number of forms. Newsletters can be used to spotlight progress being made by students, educators, or the entire school. Teachers can be asked to demonstrate resiliency-building activities that they are finding to be successful in their classrooms. Individuals who seem to be doing exceptionally well can be asked to conduct information-sharing and skill-development sessions for others.

In Conclusion

Resiliency is becoming an increasingly important issue for students, educators, and schools as a result of the number of stressors individuals commonly face, including the pace of change that is occurring across the nation and throughout the world. This reality presents educators with a challenge to do everything possible to respond to the need for resiliency building in schools. The activities suggested in this final chapter offer specific tools for educators to use in effectively facilitating resiliency-building efforts.

Assessing School Resiliency Building

Evaluate the following elements of school resiliency building using a scale of 1 to 4, with 1 indicating "we have this together," 2 indicating "we've done a lot in this area, but could do more," 3 indicating "we are getting started," and 4 indicating "nothing has been done."

Prosocial Bonding

___ *Students* have a positive bond with at least one caring adult in the school.

___ *Students* are engaged in lots of interest-based before-, after-, and during-school activities.

___ *Staff* engages in meaningful interactions with one another.

___ *Staff* has been involved in creating meaningful vision and mission statements.

___ Families are positively bonded to the *school*.

___ The physical environment of the *school* is warm, positive, and inviting.

___ TOTAL SCORE

Clear, Consistent Boundaries

___ *Students* are clear about the behaviors expected of them and experience consistency in boundary enforcement.

___ *Students* use an intervention process ("core" or "care" team) that helps them when they are having problems.

___ *Staff* is clear about what is expected of them and experience consistency of expectations.

___ *Staff* models the behavioral expectations developed for students and for adults.

___ The *school* fosters an ongoing discussion of norms, rules, goals, and expectations for staff and students.

___ The *school* provides training necessary for members of the school community to effectively set and live by behavioral expectations.

___ TOTAL SCORE

Figure 8.2. Assessing School Resiliency Building
Developed by Nan Henderson, M.S.W.

Teaching Life Skills

__ *Students* use refusal skills, assertiveness, healthy conflict resolution, good decision making and problem solving, and healthy stress-management skills most of the time.

__ *Students* are engaged in cooperative learning that focuses on both social skills and academic outcomes.

__ *Staff* works cooperatively together and emphasizes the importance of cooperation.

__ *Staff* has the interpersonal skills necessary to engage in effective organizational functioning and the professional skills necessary for effective teaching.

__ The *school* provides the skill development needed by all members of the school community.

__ The *school* promotes a philosophy of lifelong learning.

__ TOTAL SCORE

Caring and Support

__ *Students* feel cared for and supported in the school.

__ *Students* experience many types of incentives, recognitions, and rewards.

__ *Staff* feels cared for and appreciated in the school.

__ *Staff* experiences many types of incentives, recognitions, and rewards.

__ The *school* has a climate of kindness and encouragement.

__ Resources needed by students and staff are secured and distributed fairly in the *school*.

__ TOTAL SCORE

High Expectations

__ *Students* believe that they can succeed.

__ *Students* experience little or no labeling (formally or informally) or tracking.

__ *Staff* believes members can succeed.

__ *Staff* is rewarded for risk taking and excellence (e.g., merit pay).

Figure 8.2. *(continued)*

__ The *school* provides growth plans for staff and students with clear outcomes, regular reviews, and supportive feedback.

__ An attitude of "can do" permeates the *school*.

__ TOTAL SCORE

Opportunities for Meaningful Participation

__ *Students* are involved in programs that emphasize service to other students, school, and the community.

__ *Students* are involved in school decision making, including governance and policy.

__ *Staff* is involved in school decision making, including governance and policy.

__ *Staff* is engaged in both job-specific and organizationwide responsibilities.

__ Everyone in the *school* community (students, parents, staff) is viewed as resources rather than problems, objects, or clients.

__ The *school* climate emphasizes "doing what really matters" and risk taking.

__ TOTAL SCORE

__ OVERALL ASSESSMENT SCORE (total of each of the six sections)

Student _____ (total of the first two scores in each section)
Staff _____ (total of the second two scores in each section)
School _____ (total of the last two scores in each section)

Range of scores: overall, 36–144; each section, 6–24; students, staff, and the school, 12–48. Lower scores indicate positive resilience building; higher scores indicate a need for improvement.

Figure 8.2. Continued

Educator Plateauing Survey

Select the response that best completes each item, using a scale of 1 to 5, with 1 indicating "strongly agree," 2 indicating "agree," 3 indicating "undecided," 4 indicating "disagree," and 5 indicating "strongly disagree."

1. __ The realities of my job come close to matching my initial expectations.

2. __ I have high professional regard for those in leadership positions in my organization's structure.

3. __ I feel trapped because I am unable to advance in my organization.

4. __ My work is satisfying to me.

5. __ I feel burdened with the many things I am responsible for in my life.

6. __ I am bored in my current job.

7. __ I usually start a new day with a sense of enthusiasm.

8. __ To the extent that I am interested, I have opportunities to advance in my organization.

9. __ Work is the most important thing in my life.

10. __ My job is full of repetitive tasks.

11. __ I feel like I have been passed over when advancement opportunities have occurred in my organization.

12. __ I can usually find time to engage in leisure activities that I enjoy.

13. __ I have little interest in advancing within my organization's structure.

14. __ My life is too predictable.

15. __ I participate in challenging and meaningful activities in my job.

16. __ I believe I can achieve my career goals within my organization's structure.

Figure 8.3. Assessing Educator Plateauing
Developed by Mike Milstein, Ph.D.

17. __ I have been in my job too long.

18. __ I find myself being impatient too often with family and friends.

19. __ I wish I had more opportunities to advance in my organization so I could do more meaningful work.

20. __ I know my job too well.

21. __ I rarely think of my life as boring.

22. __ Although I would like to advance in my organization, given my abilities, my present position is the highest I can realistically attain in my organization.

23. __ My job affords me little opportunity to learn new things.

24. __ I am energized by the challenges and opportunities in my job.

25. __ I consider myself a risk taker in my approach to life.

26. __ Advancing further in my organization's structure would require that I give up many of the things I really like about my current position.

27. __ I feel I perform successfully in my current job.

28. __ My family and friends get irritated with me for being more involved with work than I am with other aspects of my life.

29. __ My life is turning out as well as I hoped it would.

30. __ I relate career success to promotion within my organization's structure.

Educator Plateauing Survey Scoring Sheet

The numbers in Categories A, B, and C below correspond to the 30 statements in the Plateauing Survey. Transfer your responses to the blanks provided.

Note: Those numbers that are followed by an asterisk (*) are reverse scoring items. For these items, a score of 1 should be entered as 5, a 2 becomes 4, 3 remains 3, 4 becomes 2, 5 becomes 1. *Be sure to reverse these items as noted.*

Figure 8.3. Continued

Category A	Category B	Category C
1. _____	2. _____	3. _____ *
4. _____	3. _____ *	7. _____
6. _____ *	8. _____	9. _____ *
10. _____ *	11. _____ *	12. _____
15. _____	13. _____	14. _____ *
17. _____ *	16. _____	18. _____ *
20. _____ *	19. _____ *	21. _____
23. _____ *	22. _____ *	25. _____
24. _____	26. _____	28. _____ *
27. _____	30. _____ *	29. _____

Category Totals (add each column):   *Plateau Area:*

A = _____   (Divide by 10 = _____)   Content (work has become routine)

B = _____   (Divide by 10 = _____)   Structure (sense organization doesn't offer opportunity for growth or promotion)

C = _____   (Divide by 10 = _____)   Life (feeling that life is too predictable or not fulfilling)

All Categories   (Divide by 10 = _____)   OVERALL PLATEAUING

The higher the score in each category and overall, the higher the level of plateauing. This survey can be used to assess the need for resiliency building in any of the three categories or overall.

Figure 8.3. Continued

Resiliency-Building Factors	What would it look like, feel like, sound like?		How will we know we've succeeded in achieving this resiliency builder?	
	For students	For staff	For students	For staff
1. Increase bonds				
2. Set clear, consistent boundaries				
3. Teach life skills				
4. Provide all students and staff with caring and support				
5. Provide all students and staff with high expectations for success				
6. Provide all students and staff with opportunities for meaningful participation and contribution				

Figure 8.4. Worksheet for Evaluating Resiliency Building

What measures should we use?		Who should we use them with?		When should we use them?	
For students	For staff	For students	For staff	For students	For staff

Figure 8.4. Continued

Annotated Bibliographies

Annotated Bibliography: Resiliency

The following selected annotations are offered to assist readers who wish to explore the topic of resiliency in more detail.

Benard, B. (1991). *Fostering resiliency in kids: Protective factors in the family, school, and community.* Portland, OR: Western Regional Center for Drug-Free Schools and Communities, Northwest Educational Laboratory.

This is the seminal publication on fostering resiliency in children and youth. It synthesizes more than 100 studies and articles connected to resiliency, showing how the protective factors of caring and support, high expectations, and opportunities for meaningful participation in families, schools, and communities foster resiliency.

Benard, B. (1993). *Turning the corner from risk to resiliency.* Portland, OR: Western Regional Center for Drug-Free Schools and Communities, Northwest Educational Laboratory.

This publication is a compilation of several shorter articles on resiliency published between 1991 and 1993 in the Western Center News. *The articles provide an excellent synthesis of information on*

122

several resiliency-related topics, including peer programs, collaboration, multicultural issues, school restructuring, mentoring, and others, and are a good resource for inservice and training.

Henderson, N., & Kinderwater, D. (1994). *How schools are creating resilient children: The Albuquerque Public Schools Early Opportunities Project* (video). Albuquerque, NM: Albuquerque Public Schools Team Action for Student Assistance.

This video illustrates how several elementary schools are implementing the six resiliency-building factors detailed in this book, with an emphasis on the integration of resiliency-building with school restructuring. It includes interviews about resiliency building with students, parents, teachers, and administrators. It also outlines the Albuquerque districtwide resiliency-focused project, Early Opportunities. Originally produced by Albuquerque Public Schools, the video is now available from Nan Henderson & Associates.

Higgins, G. O. (1994). *Resilient adults: Overcoming a cruel past.* San Francisco: Jossey-Bass.

Higgins conducted interviews with and administered psychological tests to 40 adults who endured severe abuse and trauma as children, yet are doing well today by several measures. This book is a compilation of what she learned and includes specific profiles of resilient adults and specific advice "from the resilient" on fostering resiliency.

Richardson, G. E., Neiger, B. L., Jensen, S., & Kumpfer, K. L. (1990). The resiliency model. *Health Education, 21*(6), 33-39.

This article is another seminal work on resiliency, also synthesizing a number of perspectives on resiliency from various social sciences. It presents the best model of the development of resiliency to date (included in chapter 1 of this book). The potential value of adversity to individual growth is emphasized.

Werner, E. E., & Smith, R. S. (1992). *Overcoming the odds: High-risk children from birth to adulthood.* New York: Cornell University Press.

Werner is known as the "Mother of Resiliency" because of her initiation and continuation with coauthor Smith of the longest resiliency-related study to date in the U.S. This book documents in reader-friendly detail the results of her 40-year longitudinal study on the Island of Kauai and includes chapters on resilient teen mothers, resilient "delinquents," and resilient youth with mental health diagnoses. It offers specific information on how children bounce back, based on the Kauai study as well as similar studies in the U.S. and elsewhere.

Wolin, S. J., & Wolin, S. (1993). *The resilient self: How survivors of troubled families rise above adversity.* New York: Villard.

The Wolins "fill out" the picture of how individuals react to growing up under adversity, pointing out with compassion the strengths ("resiliencies" described in chapter 1 of this book) that also develop while dealing with painful situations. They challenge the popular culture's emphasis on "survivor as victim," and emphasize the importance of moving from a Damage Model to a Challenge Model of viewing the outcomes of adversity.

Wolin, S. J., & Wolin, S. (1994). *Survivor's pride: Building resilience in youth at risk* (video). Vernona, WI: Attainment Company.

In the first part of this video, the Wolins present the seven "resiliencies" described in their book and the difference between the Damage Model and the Challenge Model. Most of the video, however, is in-depth interviews with resilient young people and the adults in their lives who are fostering their resiliency. This video is useful as an inspiring training resource for any group who works with youth.

Annotated Bibliography: School Change and School Restructuring

The following annotations are offered to assist readers who wish to explore effective school change, organizational development, and restructuring in more detail.

Fiske, E. B. (1992). *Smart schools, smart kids*. New York: Simon & Schuster.

This book surveys the educational landscape, offering several de-tailed examples of exceptional schools that embody the best of school reform and resiliency building. It offers readers valuable insights that can help them improve their own schools and includes a "Resource Guide to Smart Schools."

Fullan, M. G. (1991). *The meaning of educational change* (2nd ed.). New York: Teachers College Press.

This seminal book on school change provides a solid foundation for understanding change and innovation in education. Causes, plan-ning, and processes connected to effective change are included. Particular emphasis is placed on teachers, principals, students, district administrators, consultants, and communities as they re-late to school change.

Herman, J. L., Aschbacher, P. R., & Winters, L. (1992). *A practical guide to alternative assessment*. Alexandria, VA: Association for Super-vision and Curriculum Development.

This guide to effective assessment, which is written in practitioner language, encourages readers to focus on things that are important rather than things that can be counted. It also encourages readers to create their own assessment tools and provides specific ideas for instrument development.

Meier, D. (1995). *The power of their ideas*. Boston: Beacon.

For 20 years Meier has led a school that defies the stereotypes of public education—Central Park East in Harlem, where 90% of the students graduate and 90% of those go on to college. She offers personal and professional reflections on the success of her school, describing the innovations used—all of which are reflections of resiliency building. She also argues eloquently for similar innova-tions to take place in education in general.

Milstein, M. (1993). *Restructuring schools: Doing it right.* Newbury Park, CA: Corwin.

This book is a practitioner guide to school restructuring, which breaks the process of effective school change into practical, easy-to-understand steps. It includes information on how to develop structures and roles to accomplish restructuring and offers activities to use in the effort. Each important part of the process is diagrammed in a graphic model, which further clarifies how restructuring occurs.

Murphy, J., & Hallinger, P. (1993). *Restructuring schooling: Learning from ongoing efforts.* Newbury Park, CA: Corwin.

This book includes a background and definition of restructuring, as well as a useful categorization of the various elements that should be considered in the process. Emphasis is given to the "core technology" of curriculum and instruction. A realistic perspective is offered regarding implementation issues.

National LEADership Network Study Group on Restructuring Schools. (1991). Washington, DC: U.S. Department of Education.

A group composed of LEAD directors from nine states, and others, examines the education and training that school leaders require to be able to guide restructuring. Based on feedback from administrators involved in restructuring, the report emphasizes leadership development and changing leadership role expectations.

Schmuck, R., & Runkel, P. J. (1994). *The handbook of organization development in schools and colleges.* Prospect Heights, IL: Waveland.

Restructuring ultimately depends on schools' capacities for change and renewal. This book introduces the technology of organization development and presents in practical terms techniques for conducting such activities as assessment, survey feedback, intervention, and evaluation. In addition, it examines goal setting, communications, problem solving, decision making, and other group effectiveness concerns and suggests activities for improvement.

References

Anderson, G., Herr, K., & Nihlen, A. (1994). *Studying your own school.* Thousand Oaks, CA: Corwin.

Bardwick, J. (1986). *Plateauing.* New York: Amacom.

Benard, B. (1991). *Fostering resiliency in kids: Protective factors in the family, school, and community.* Portland, OR: Western Regional Center for Drug-Free Schools and Communities, Northwest Educational Laboratory.

Benard, B. (1993). *Turning the corner from risk to resiliency.* Portland, OR: Western Regional Center for Drug-Free Schools and Communities, Northwest Educational Laboratory.

Berman, P., & McLaughlin, M. (1977). *Federal programs supporting educational change: Vol. 7. Factors affecting implementation and continuation.* Santa Monica, CA: RAND.

Botvin, G. J., & Botvin, E. M. (1992). Adolescent tobacco, alcohol, and drug abuse: Prevention strategies, empirical findings, and assessment issues. *Journal of Developmental and Behavioral Pediatrics, 13*(4), 29.

Bowers, D. J., & Franklin, J. L. (1977). *Survey-guided development I: Data-based organizational change.* La Jolla, CA: University Associates.

Boyer, E. L. (1983). *High schools: A report on secondary education in America.* New York: Harper & Row.

Cameron, J. (1992). *The artist's way: A spiritual path to higher creativity.* New York: The Putnam Publishing Group.

Cooper, C., & Henderson, N. (1995). *Motivating schools to change: Integrating the threads of school restructuring.* Tasmania, Australia: Global Learning Communities.

Covey, S. R. (1989). *The seven habits of highly effective people.* New York: Simon & Schuster.

Deal, T. (1987). The culture of schools. In Association for Supervision and Curriculum Development, 1987 yearbook: *Leadership.* Alexandria, VA: Association for Supervision and Curriculum Development.

Duncan, A. (1995). Caring classroom nurtures children's resilience. *Western Center News, 8*(2) 1, 3.

Fine, M. (1991). *Framing dropouts: Notes on the politics of the urban public high school.* Albany: State University of New York Press.

Fiske, E. B. (1992). *Smart schools, smart kids.* New York: Simon & Schuster.

Fullan, M. G. (1991). *The meaning of educational change* (2nd ed.). New York: Teachers College Press.

Gelham, D. (1991). The miracle of resiliency. *Newsweek* (Special Issue), Summer, 44-47.

Goodlad, J. (1983). A place called school: Prospects for the future. New York: McGraw-Hill.

Hawkins, J. D., & Catalano, R. F. (1990). *20 questions: Adolescent substance abuse risk factors* (Audiotape). Seattle, WA: Developmental Research and Programs, Inc.

Hawkins, J. D., Catalano, R. F., & Miller, J. Y. (1992). Risk and protective factors for alcohol and other drug problems. *Psychological Bulletin, 112*(1), 64-105.

Henderson, N., & Kinderwater, D. (1994). *How schools are creating resilient children: The Albuquerque Public Schools Early Opportunities Project* (Video). Albuquerque, NM: Albuquerque Public Schools Team Action for Student Assistance.

Herman, J. L., Aschbacher, P. R., & Winters, L. (1992). *A practical guide to alternative assessment.* Alexandria, VA: Association for Supervision and Curriculum Development.

Higgins, G. O. (1994). *Resilient adults: Overcoming a cruel past.* San Francisco: Jossey-Bass.

Johnson, D. W., & Johnson, R. (1989). *Cooperation and competition: Theory and research.* Edina, MN: Interactive Book Company.

Krueger, R. A. (1994). *Focus groups* (2nd ed.). Thousand Oaks, CA: Sage.

Levine, S. L. (1989). *Promoting adult growth in schools.* Boston: Allyn & Bacon.

Lightfoot, S. L. (1983). *The good high school: Portraits of character and culture.* New York: Basic Books.

McLaughlin, M., Irby, M., & Langman, J. (1994). *Urban sanctuaries: Neighborhood organizations in the lives and futures of inner-city youth.* San Francisco: Jossey-Bass.

Meier, D. (1995a, July). Small schools, big results. *The American School Board Journal,* 37-40.

Meier, D. (1995b). *The power of their ideas.* Boston: Beacon.

Milstein, M. (1990). Plateauing as an occupational phenomenon among teachers and administrators. *Journal of Personnel Evaluation in Education, 3,* 325-336.

Milstein, M. (1993). *Restructuring schools: Doing it right.* Newbury Park, CA: Corwin.

Murphy, J., & Hallinger, P. (1993). *Restructuring schooling: Learning from ongoing efforts.* Newbury Park, CA: Corwin.

Nadler, D. A. (1979). Alternative data-feedback designs for organizational intervention. In *The 1979 annual handbook for group facilitators.* La Jolla, CA: University Associates, Inc.

National Commission on Excellence in Education. (1983). *A nation at risk: The imperative for educational reform.* Washington, D.C.: U.S. Department of Education.

National LEADership Network Study Group on Restructuring Schools. (1991). Washington, DC: U.S. Department of Education.

Noddings, N. (1988). Schools face "crisis in caring." *Education Week,* December 7, p. 32.

Noddings, N. (1992). *The challenge to care in schools: An alternative approach to education.* New York: Teachers College Press.

Peters, T., & Waterman, R. (1982). *In search of excellence: Lessons from America's best-run companies.* New York: Warner Books.

Richardson, G. E., Neiger, B. L., Jensen, S., & Kumpfer, K. L. (1990). The resiliency model. *Health Education, 21*(6), 33-39.

Rirkin, M., & Hoopman, M. (1991). *Moving beyond risk to resiliency.* Minneapolis, MN: Minneapolis Public Schools.

Rosenthal, R., & Jacobson, L. (1968). *Pygmalion in the classroom.* New York: Holt, Rinehart, & Winston.

Schmuck, R., & Runkel, P. J. (1994). *The handbook of organization development in schools and colleges.* Prospect Heights, IL: Waveland.

Senge, P., Kleiner, A., Roberts, C., Ross, R. B., & Smith, B. J. (1994). *The fifth discipline fieldbook.* New York: Currency Doubleday.

Werner, E. E. (1990). Protective factors and individual resilience. In S. J. Meisels & J. Shonkoff. (Eds.), *Handbook of early childhood intervention* (pp. 97-116). New York: Cambridge University Press.

Werner, E. E., & Smith, R. S. (1992). *Overcoming the odds: High risk children from birth to adulthood.* New York: Cornell University Press.

Willower, D. J. (1965). Hypotheses on the school as a social system. *Educational Administration Quarterly, 1,* 42-51.

Wolin, S. J., & Wolin, S. (1993). *The resilient self: How survivors of troubled families rise above adversity.* New York: Villard.

Wolin, S. J., & Wolin, S. (1994). *Survivor's pride: Building resilience in youth at risk* (video). Vernona, WI: Attainment Company.

Index

**CORWIN
PRESS**

The Corwin Press logo—a raven striding across an open book—represents the happy union of courage and learning. We are a professional-level publisher of books and journals for K–12 educators, and we are committed to creating and providing resources that embody these qualities. Corwin's motto is "Success for All Learners."